ULSTER COUNTY – VIEWED FROM SUMMIT.

WITTENBERG MT. 3824 FEET   CROSS MT. 3400 FEET   SAMUELS POINT 3000 FEET.

BELLE AYRE MOUNTAIN & PINE HILL STATION.

SKETCHED FROM NATURE BY H. SCHILE.

LL MOUNTAINS N. Y.

IN CATSKILL COUNTRY

Overleaf: The upper part of the Kaaterskill Clove shown here, retains the look of forested grandeur it had in Indian days. The two summits against the sky are Round Top and High Peak, once believed to be the highest in the Catskills.

PHOTOGRAPH BY JERRY NOVESKY

IN CATSKILL COUNTRY

Collected Essays on Mountain History, Life and Lore

ALF EVERS

Introduction by Heywood Hale Broun
Foreword by Tom Hatley
Executive Director of The Catskill Center for
Conservation and Development

THE OVERLOOK PRESS

WOODSTOCK • NEW YORK

First published in the United States in 1995 by
The Overlook Press
Lewis Hollow Road
Woodstock, New York 12498

These essays first appeared in *The Catskill Center News*, published by the Catskill Center for Conservation and Development.

Library of Congress Cataloging-in-Publication Data

Evers, Alf. In Catskill Country : collected essays on mountain history, life, and lore / Alf Evers ; foreword by Tom Hatley ; introduction by Heywood H. Broun. Includes bibliographical references. 1. Catskill Mountains (N.Y.)—History. 2. Catskill Mountains (N.Y.)—Social life and customs. 3. Mountain life—New York (State)—Catskill Mountains. I. Title.
F127.C3E94 1994   974.7'38—dc20   94-18207 CIP
ISBN: 0-87951-566-X

BOOK DESIGN BY BERNARD SCHLEIFER
TYPESET BY AEROTYPE, INC.

First Edition

10 9 8 7 6 5 4 3 2 1

CONTENTS

A FEW LINES OF THANKS

IN A BOOK LIKE THE PRESENT ONE THE PERSON WHOSE NAME APPEARS on the title page as author owes a great deal to many others. There are obvious inanimate helpers such as libraries, archives, printed books and newspapers, old pictures and statistics and so on. And as in any book which hopes to catch a hint of the flavor of a region there are the words of living people met and questioned in the course of many days of wandering about the Catskills. Such words often deal with verifiable facts but often they convey elusive traditions, opinions, prejudice or other little clues to the ways in which the people of the Catskills see themselves, their home communities and the region of which their communities form a part. The people of the region whom I questioned have been generous in their answers. I can only recall one instance in which a request for information was refused. In response to a knock on the front door of her house the woman inside said, "No, I never speak to a strange man unless my husband is present and he's away at work." But after an exchange of shouts from both sides of the door the lady agreed to emerge, sit down on the porch and answer my questions while in full view of her neighbors. And her answers were intelligent and to the point. To this lady and to all the other mountain people who answered my questions—my thanks. And hearty thanks to my editor at the Catskill Center, Jerry Novesky and to Maureen Nagy, editor at The Overlook Press who worked together to overcome the difficulties that beset the guidance of nineteen scattered essays as it became a book. Finally I want to express my appreciation of Heywood Hale's Introduction and the Foreword of Tom Hatley and to express the hope that someday in the future I may become worthy of the kind thoughts about my work to which they have given utterance.

ALF EVERS
Shady, New York

FOREWORD

THE ECOLOGIST ULDIS ROZE ONCE CHARACTERIZED THE DISTINCTIVE feature of the Catskills landscape as its narrow, close-ended valleys. Not quite box canyons, they give these mountains their unique form and shape.

Alf Evers's essays are matched to their countryside. They lead us into a seemingly narrow topic, an end not too far off in sight. But they pull us out at the end to a higher perspective than that from which we began. Taken together, they add up to a series of new views on the land, lives and language of a place of unexpected complexity.

Alf Evers has been as generous to the Catskill Center for Conservation and Development as he is to his readers. He has, almost since its inception, served as a board member of the Center: considered and thoughtful advice from Alf through the years has helped the Center, now in its 25th year, better fit its programs to the Catskills. In addition, Alf contributed this memorable series of original essays to the Center's *News*. Now assembled in one volume, they are as fresh today as when originally published.

There is no better introduction to the Catskills than through Alf's eyes, welcoming all of his readers, like friends, to this piece of distinctly American landscape.

If, as a society, we valued close, reflective knowledge of our land, then we would count Alf Evers among our treasures. Through these essays one gets to know a unique place; through his generosity, a unique man.

TOM HATLEY, *Executive Director*
The Catskill Center for Conservation and Development

INTRODUCTION

ALF EVERS HAS SPENT MOST OF HIS LONG LIFE IN THE CATSKILLS, AND more than any other writer has gathered together, catalogued and recorded everything he could find out about life on the eroded mountain stumps which rise on the west bank of the Hudson.

For those settlers who traditionally depended on cultivation of the land for their livelihoods, nature's bounty would have seemed to be doled out in stingy scraps in this area. While the original Native American hunters and gatherers revered the mountains' slopes and forests as important hunting grounds, later settlers would come to consider the Catskills a challenging place to make a living. One old-time farmer of these slopes paid his respects to them by remarking to Evers, "Where there's two stones to every dirt, you're in the Catskills."

Not many farmers among early European settlers were lucky enough to land on the soft, rich hills across the Hudson or on the flatlands bordering the Esopus Creek. Many had to make do as tenant farmers of stony Catskill Mountain farms owned by absentee landlords who lived in style along the east bank of the Hudson or in New York City. The settlers put to use the mountains' dense stands of hemlock by using the timber as long walls and bark roofs of their simple cabins; a later generation peeled hemlock bark for use in tanning leather. Still others attacked the mountains' rocky ribs as quarriers of bluestone to be sent down the Hudson on sloops or barges to build the harsh new cities of the industrial age. And more recently, dwellers in the Catskills subsisted on serving the tourists who came to gaze at the beauty which is often the bright side of rugged terrain.

When reading Evers's work I am reminded of old Gilbert White, the 18th century English clergyman whose territory— the parish of Selborne—was smaller than Alf's mountain range but which, in *The Natural History* and *Antiquities of Selborne*, produced a book still in print after almost two centuries.

White in his time, as Evers in his, proved that a detailed examination of a world small enough for the imagination to encompass has the fascination one might get by looking through the tube of some celestial macro-microscope at the threads of a moving tapestry.

"It has been my misfortune," wrote White, "never to have had any neighbor whose studies have led him toward the pursuit of natural knowledge." No such problem affected the gregarious Evers, who will wade through a swamp of repetitive chat with a garrulous ancient to emerge with a nugget of interesting lore. You may not know when viper's bugloss first grew beside the Sawkill River, but Alf Evers found out for you, discovered that it used to be called Betsey Bigelow's flower, found out who Ms. Bigelow was, and makes you interested in the whole business.

The interest is in the whole continuum of change evoked by these pieces: the progression from the silence of the early hemlock forest, through the sound of axes, of trains, of oars and to the hush that has once again descended in places where the hemlock has returned.

In one of the last essays in this collection, Evers speaks lovingly of an early teacher, an amateur anthropologist named Byron Terwilliger who carefully collected kegs full of those flint fragments with which the first Americans killed game, skinned it and, more peaceably, carved softer materials into now-lost works of art. The stone bits that the old teacher collected are mid-way steps in the long development, rise, fall, rise, fall of the Catskills, as nature's preserve, as man's, as an uneasy sharing between occupiers and the occupied territory.

Rip Van Winkle slept in the Catskills to wake and find things vastly changed. Alf Evers, ever wakeful, has mixed a scholar's detachment with a lover's warmth in recording these changes.

Wordsworth once rebuked an ancestor of mine—"Degenerate Douglas" he bitingly called him—for sending forth

"Word, to level with the dust a noble horde,
A brotherhood of venerable trees."

Wordsworth was, however, as far-seeing as Alf Evers, and ended the poem with the upbeat words

"Sheltered places, bosoms, nooks and bays,
and the pure mountains and the gentle Tweed
And the green silent pastures, yet remain."

Alf Evers knows the Catskills as they were, as they are, and as
he hopes they'll be.

HEYWOOD HALE BROUN

In late spring the blossoms of a shad tree light up the Valley as it stands above a garden of domesticated and clipped hemlocks mixed with deciduous trees clinging to a precipitous slope with a boisterous mountain stream below.
AUTHOR'S PHOTOGRAPH

THE LORE OF A
HEMLOCK VALLEY

MORE THAN THIRTY YEARS AGO, I MOVED FROM a house on a sunny mountainside where oaks flourished above cleared fields to another house in the Catskills set in a deep and narrow valley. There, hemlock trees dotted the deciduous woods that rose on rocky tiers behind my old house in the hamlet of Shady. Across the bustling stream called the Sawkill, other hemlocks did their best to keep a foothold on a high and steep bank of treacherous glacial clays and gravels. An occasional tree, pushed too hard by wind and water, tumbled into the stream, setting off a miniature avalanche of clay and boulders.

At the eastern end of my place stood a small grove of hemlocks. The older hemlocks there grew tall and straight; their lower branches had died away from a lack of sunlight. The grove reminded me strongly of the one John Burroughs had written about in his essay, "In the Hemlocks." It had the same rich bird life, the same surrounding zone of varied plants. The first time I saw the grove, I heard a ruffed grouse rising up from a springy spot on the grove's edge.

In his essay, Burroughs wrote about the assaults on the Catskills' hemlocks of barkpeelers and lumbermen, and of settlers eager for cleared fields on which grain might be grown or cows pastured. He wrote of the resistance of the hemlocks, of their ability to hold their own under difficult conditions. When I moved to my house beside the Sawkill, I saw my hemlock neighbors putting up the same resistance. And I learned that the hemlocks could help me understand the past of my neighborhood—all I had to do was to keep my eyes open and to ask the right questions.

I knew before I settled down in Shady that the valley had once been the site of a busy glassmaking operation which lasted for nearly half a century. I knew that the glassmakers had cut every hardwood tree in sight to feed their furnaces, and that when hardwoods grew scarce, they had resorted to hemlock. I knew that sawmills had stood at a number of good mill sites in the valley and had reduced to boards and planks every tree within reach that might yield a sawlog.

Yet, in spite of this, I could see that the forests that had once filled the valley were returning, and that the hemlocks were asserting a dominance they owed to their close adaptation to local conditions. On the hillsides in my part of the valley, the former community of native American plants was becoming well established.

In the narrow valley bottom beside the road and the Sawkill, however, immigrant plants that had accompanied early settlers were doing well and had crowded out many native ones. I asked old-timers whether the immigrant coltsfoot, which every spring opens its dandelion-like blossoms on recently exposed subsoil beside the Sawkill, had been common in their youth—they couldn't remember that it had.

They did better when I asked whether the member of the borage family known as viper's bugloss had formed part of their childhood existence. "Yes it had," an old-timer said, "only we called it Betsey Bigelow's flower." And who was Betsey Bigelow? I asked. "Why, she'd lived in the valley when glassmaking was the big thing. When the glassmakers left, Betsey remained behind. She lived alone in a little cabin on the hillside to the west of the road. That's why we call the hillside Betsey Bigelow's." And what about the flower, I asked. "Oh, it was seen for the very first time in this valley beside Betsey's cabin—no one ever knew how it got there. And so people gave it her name."

Hemlocks mixed with maples, ash, and birch long ago recaptured Betsey Bigelow's hill. Heaps of stones gathered from eroding plowed fields, massive stone walls, and the character of the face of the soil told of how the hillside, steep as it was, had once been plowed and planted to corn and rye, and, as the soil washed away, to less-demanding buckwheat. After even buckwheat asked too much of it, the hillside became a cow pasture. I traced the old pasture enclosures and saw that where stone walls were lacking, fence wire had been strung half a century ago. Parallel marks on the trunk of a double hemlock standing on my boundary line showed that the tree had been used as a living fence post. I looked up the tree's trunk and felt a bit puzzled, for its once-graceful lower branches had all been sawed off. No explanation I could think of satisfied me. So I asked my neighbor. And his answer surprised me.

My neighbor had been working on his well-kept place several decades ago when a man from high on Hutchin Hill came by and asked if he could have a few hours' work. He didn't want much, he said, just enough to finance the purchase of a bottle of wine. At first my neighbor said there wasn't anything he needed done. Then he looked at the hillside and saw the double hemlock still in possession of its lower branches. All the trees around my neighbor's house had been subjected, as was the local custom, to a process called "trimming up," This gave the trees a cared-for look and allowed grass to grow right up to their bases.

The double hemlock had escaped this treatment because it stood so far from its owner's house. But now its turn came. With a saw in his hand, the wine lover climbed the hillside and attacked the double hemlock's lower branches. When he had cut away enough branches to produce the price of his bottle, he stopped, collected his pay and hastened to town to slake his thirst. Since I learned this bit of lore I have thought of the double hemlock as belonging to a species unknown to botanists—the *Tsuga vinifera*, or wine hemlock.

Stimulated by what I had learned from the wine hemlock, I became sensitized to hemlocks in general, and I began seeing hemlock lore everywhere. I realized then that I lived in a kind of hemlock box: the mortised-and-tenoned framework of my house was of hemlock, so were my oldest floors, so was the siding; the lath beneath the plaster walls had been made of thin hemlock board split with a hatchet and then pulled out like an accordion. I learned that the glasshouses and workers' cottages of long ago had been built of hemlock. I learned that a dam of hemlock logs had held back the waters of a millpond and that the water had run through a hemlock flume on its way to the mill wheel of a wood-turning mill. Then the same water, emerging from the mill's tailrace, had made its way via another hemlock flume to turn the wheel of an up-and-down hemlock sawmill about a thousand feet from the turning mill. On its way to the sawmill, the water had powered a primitive washing machine in the basement of the mill owner's house.

I began to experiment with the many ways in which the hemlock can be used. I made a hemlock garden of trimmed trees and seedlings, some rearranged to form a circle on a little plateau above my house. Chickadees like to spend cold winter nights in these hemlocks; the circle has grown dense enough to become a good place for human sunbathing on cold and windy days. On top of a high rocky outcropping, I built a shelter of hemlock logs to which I might climb from my valley house and look out over the world of mountains and blue distance.

On every occasion that I have visited the small hemlock grove near my house, I have felt refreshed by its peacefulness and fascinated, as John Burroughs had been, by the birds and the low, native plants that gather around a stand of hemlocks—the trilliums, jack-in-the-pulpits, star flowers, club mosses, ferns, mountain laurel, and others. And I wondered how it had happened that the grove had managed to survive in this hemlock-hungry and sawmill-rich valley. As in the case of the wine tree, I asked questions and I got my answer—it led to a man very different from the wine drinker.

My hemlock grove grows from a moraine strewn with huge boulders put there some 10,000 years ago as the last glacial ice sheet retreated. Directly below and down a series of rocky ledges stand a house and barn that once belonged to a man named Shaffer Vosburgh. Vosburgh and his brother ran the family wood-turning mill across the road. There he spent his long, working life making balusters, porch pillars, table and chair legs, and other turned stuff of local hardwood.

Outside the mill, however, Vosburgh had interests unrelated to wood turning. As one of his daughters wrote,

> although . . . nurtured in a small obscure Valley in the Catskill Mountains. . . . He grew up to be comfortably at home in the universe and in love with life in general . . . the wonders of creation thrilled him, the mystery of the seasons, an eclipse of the sun; the *aurora borealis* over our hemlock hill. . . . He would often take us from our work to view some wonder he had discovered, perhaps . . . a spider web in the sun. . . .

He would hold a toad in his hand while gently stroking its head, or hold a wasp and observe it, confident that it would not sting him. Touchy horses and dogs became mild and friendly in his presence. He liked to stand at the backdoor of his house and feed birds from his hand. The birds came down from the safety of his hemlock hill—the very same place that I now think of as my hemlock grove.

From time to time, lumbermen asked Vosburgh to sell the trees on the hemlock hill, but he always refused. He wanted the hemlocks to remain as they were because they meant so much to the birds. Vosburgh died more than forty years ago, yet the hemlocks he so greatly valued remain. Older trees die and younger ones take their places as the grove delights people of our own time. And I hope it will live on to delight people of the future.

As I explored the life and history of my neighborhood with the aid of hemlock trees and other plants, I was led into solving many little mysteries which helped give me a deepened sense of the interrelatedness of plants and humans. Yet I did not solve all local hemlock mysteries.

One stormy day, the Sawkill flooded. Directly opposite my house, it tore out its bed and revealed a construction of timbers about five feet down. The timbers were hemlock logs, fitted together to form a dam. No one I asked, not even the oldest inhabitant, had ever heard of this dam. Although the logs, from all evidence, must have been in place for at least a century-and-a-half, their water-soaked condition had kept them from decaying, and they were almost as good as new.

No old maps or records and no local traditions have shed any light on the origin of the dam exposed by the flood. Yet I feel confident that someday I may stumble on a clue that may lead me to its builder, and so enlarge my understanding of human and plant life in this hemlock valley. Meanwhile, a flood has covered the old dam deep in boulders and preserved it so that future inhabitants of the hemlock valley may discover it after another great flood has come along.

Log cabins of this type were built as bunkhouses for barkpeelers working for mountain tanneries between 1815-1860. This one in Woodland Valley became ruinous as tanning ended and was roughly restored as an artist's summer retreat c. 1890. PHOTOGRAPH C. 1902, AUTHOR'S COLLECTION

WITH BROADAX
AND POLL AX

Back in July 1961, old George Shultis of Wittenberg in the town of Woodstock was expressing his feelings about the high cost of lumber—he'd just had to pay a dollar for two pieces of two-by-four.

"If I was as young as I used to be," said George, "I'd take a broadax and a poll ax into the woods and I'd hew me a house." George had helped build several log houses in his youth, and when he was young he'd gotten his mail at a log post office. Many people living in all parts of the forested Catskills have threatened to hew their own log houses, and a few have gone ahead and done it, while many have made do with prefabricated imitations. The urge to live within log walls is still strong in the Catskills.

By the time the Catskills were being settled by white people, the log cabin had spread from beginnings in Delaware and Pennsylvania and was becoming a part of American frontier tradition. By 1875, when framed houses were thrusting log ones aside in the region, the New York State Census reported 851 inhabited log houses in the four Catskills counties. This figure did not include many abandoned ones or those disguised with a coat of weatherboarding or absorbed into more modern structures.

Many bits of information that made their way into the older town and county histories of the Catskills tell us that settlers often began by putting up a frame of crotched sticks set in the earth and covered with evergreen boughs or sheets of bark. Others dug bark-roofed shelters into well-drained hillsides, and some followed the Indians or Native Americans and made dome-shaped or elongated shelters of saplings and bark. These were temporary shelters and as soon as possible a log house was built.

Log houses were of two kinds. One was the traditional log cabin that plays so large a part in our folklore; it was built of round logs with notched joints and projections at the corners. The other and more elegant was known as a "blockhouse"–its name and type derived from military structures long used in Europe.

Catskill Mountain blockhouses were put together from squared logs with dovetailed or overlapping joints and flush corners. Roofs of both types were at first of sheets of bark, often elm or ash, held down (because of the prevailing high cost of nails) with poles secured with fastenings of tough and limber vines. Later, hand-made shingles came into use–they were often three feet long and were laid one foot to the weather. The logs–of hemlock, pine, spruce, or hardwoods–were chinked with splinters of wood embedded in clay. In the rudest cabins–those described by travelers as "log huts"—the chimney was a hole in the roof; more pretentious log houses had chimneys made of sticks and clay set above a jambless fireplace. Eventually, stone chimneys took over, and destructive fires became less frequent.

The door of some cabins was no more than an old woolen blanket which might be replaced as settlement prospered by a wooden door with wooden hinges and a wooden latch. When floors were not of earth they were of logs split and laid with the flat side uppermost.

In the early nineteenth century, log houses outnumbered framed ones in the more isolated Catskills towns and hamlets—this was the case in the 1820s in Liberty and in Griffin's Corners, among others.

Log structures sheltered more than just households: there were many log taverns—one in Sullivan County was described as consisting of a "double blockhouse" with the largest pair of deer antlers ever found in the region ornamenting the facade; log schoolhouses were the rule in some towns; workers in early industries such as tanning and glassmaking were often housed in log buildings; log houses served to hold religious meetings before proper churches could be built; logs were set to work to form pens for enclosing farm animals and occasionally for a small barn; and "hoopshavers" often shaved their barrel hoops in log huts with a huge stone fireplace at one end to consume the shavings. In 1845, when Anti-Renters were being arrested at a fast clip, three log jails were set up in Delhi by the militia to hold prisoners pending trial.

By the time the census takers of 1875 got to work, log houses had become romantic. While advantageous

to political climbers (wishing to ape the humble beginnings of a then-recent president), they were of no use
at all to social climbers, usually being shelters for the
poor. Shortly thereafter, log houses of a new kind rose
to high favor among prosperous and sophisticated
Americans as a log-and-bark revival got underway.
The revival owed much to a nostalgia for frontier days
and its foremost symbol, the log cabin. And it owed a
great deal to romantic European models of the eighteenth and early nineteenth centuries. Logs, half logs,
peeled, or, in Henry Thoreau's words, left "with the
fur on," slabs from the local sawmill, poles, oddly
shaped malformations of branches, trunks and roots,
and roughly sawed boards were woven into structures
with what was felt as a wild and rustic effect. Many of
the Catskills' residential parks shared in the revival; so
too did such buildings as George Gould's "log palace"
at Furlough Lake.

John Burroughs, the most eloquent celebrator of
the Catskills, shared this love for log buildings, as did
Thoreau and other nature students. When he built his
rustic retreat called Slabsides in 1895, he covered it with
bark-covered slabs that suggested the log cabin his
grandparents had built in Delaware County a century
earlier, and he ornamented its interior with woodwork
and furniture he made himself of unpeeled yellow
birch and other local woods.

It is easy to understand the appeal of buildings
hewn, in George Shultis's words, with broadax and
poll ax. Such buildings in their vigorous contours and
shapes relate well to their surrounding earth, rocks,
and forest. The texture of their walls does far less visual

violence to a natural environment than the smooth, painted surfaces of grander buildings. There are probably more early log houses still standing among the Catskills than we realize, although they are hidden behind modern embellishments, as is the one known as Cabin John, built in the 1820s in the town of Olive. These and the buildings of the log-and-bark revival had important parts in the Catskills' cultural and social history—and they deserve to be kept alive and well.

For forty years the great American actor Joseph Jefferson played the role of Rip Van Winkle to delighted audiences around the world. This photograph was taken c. 1885 by New York's famous firm of Sarony and Major. As used here, it is from a pirated version printed in Leipzig, Germany, c. 1908.

AUTHOR'S COLLECTION

RIP'S SECOND
LONG SLEEP

OR WELL OVER A CENTURY AFTER RIP VAN WIN-
kle was born in the imagination of Washington Irving, he reigned as the guardian spirit
of the Catskills. He became a nineteenth-
century version of similar spirits in many
parts of the world who were linked to springs, mountains, cities, and plains. For example, the ancient Romans believed many localities were under the care of
what they knew as a *genius loci*, or "genius of the place."

At the height of Rip's spectacular career as "the
genius" or guardian spirit of the Catskills, the mountains seemed to have taken on many of the characteris-
tics Irving had given to Rip. Like Rip, the Catskills
came to seem a relaxed region where conventional
ways of living might be thrown aside and where a love
of nature and of hunting and fishing colored most
aspects of existence. Rip was a fellow of dreamy and
impractical notions—the Catskills acquired the same
disposition and so clothed themselves in a colorful and
romantic veil.

The popularity of the Catskills' summer resorts owed a good deal to Rip's presence. As late as June 14, 1953, the *New York Times* headlined a story about the resorts of the Catskills with "The Vacationland Rip Van Winkle Built." But by that time, Rip's hold on the Catskills was slipping and the old fellow was once more becoming drowsy. His wakeful moments, however, should not be forgotten.

In the 1730s, poet Alexander Pope had advised designers of gardens to consult "the Genius of the Place" as they made their plans. This was just what resort owners in the Catskills once tried to do. They invoked Rip at every turn: they marked the rock on which he'd had his twenty-year sleep and the trail he'd followed; they put to work buildings that they assured the willing public had some imagined sort of connection with Rip, and they named new hotels and boardinghouses in his honor or in that of his creator, Washington Irving. Rip's picture as a bearded old man awakening from his long sleep decorated the timetables of railroads leading to the Catskills. A Hudson River steamboat was named for him, and murals celebrating Rip's marvelous history became a feature of a steamboat named the *Washington Irving*.

At first, Rip presided over no more than the vicinity of the Catskill Mountain House, near which he was rumored to have had his famous sleep. But as the years passed, Rip's domain grew until it included all of the Catskills.

Rip's position as "the genius" of the Catskills was given a big boost by the worldwide success of *Rip Van Winkle*, the play that Joseph Jefferson and Dion Boucicault based on Irving's tale. In the play, the spirits of Henry Hudson's crew—whom Rip had watched bowling among the Catskills—became gnome-like beings. The play took on romantic and melodramatic turns that would have astonished Irving, but which made the Catskills more than ever a land of magic. And in the play, Rip lost much of what we think of as his male chauvinist look, and his shrewish wife, Gretchen, became a more credible character.

At one time, the owners of Catskill Mountain resorts honored Rip by building bowling alleys and by selling liquor that might affect visitors as remarkably as had the gin Rip had drunk in Irving's tale. But as the twentieth century took shape, many bowling alleys were replaced by tennis courts and golf links, in which Rip could have had no interest. The coming of Prohibition closed bars in the region and turned drinking into a furtive and sometimes hazardous pursuit. By the 1920s, Rip's bearded face had disappeared from timetables and promotional leaflets. Postcards featuring Rip were still being sold, but more and more cards showing cats engaged in many appealing activities were competing with Rip.

About 1960, I asked the publicity man for a group of mountain resorts why he didn't use Rip in his advertising. The man smiled indulgently at me as if I were some sleepy backwoodsman who had just stumbled out into the real world. "Today," the man said, "we are projecting a new image for the Catskills. Progress, you know." I realized that the man was right.

For decades the new image had been building up as Rip grew ever drowsier. Old hotels and boardinghouses had been shedding their verandahs and throwing out their old furniture made in mountain shops. Rag carpeting woven by local housewives had been displaced by the products of distant factories. Cows no longer grazed within sight of boardinghouse guests, and chickens had ceased cackling in nearby barnyards. At the urging of resort owners, new highways had been driven through the mountains, shoving aside old houses and picturesque inns, removing curves that enhanced the charm of the landscape and interfering with the free flow of trout streams. The Catskills of Rip Van Winkle were fading out, and the new image was being put in place. If all went well, before long the Catskills would look and feel as much as possible like anywhere else.

All this change had not happened without resistance. Outside the Catskills, Rip was still accepted as the region's guardian spirit. As one writer put it in 1930, to "untold thousands of citizens," Rip and his story were "the beginning and the end of all they knew about the Catskills." Within the region, too, Rip had his loyal supporters who continued to name an occasional business venture for him. A bridge bearing his name went up in 1935, across the Hudson River. And an old dream of annual performances of *Rip Van Winkle* in the Catskills lived on.

In the 1950s, a puppet-show version of the play was being given at Rip's Retreat at North Lake and close to what was generally accepted as the site of Rip's great adventure in sleeping. The Retreat featured a mock village of Rip's time, with attendants and craft workers in costume. An imitation railway circled the

Retreat, and a bearded actor impersonated Rip. Rip's Retreat had been planned to give off a Walt Disney-like air—Disney himself is said to have expressed approval of it but, faced with many difficulties, the venture failed.

The next try at reviving Rip also leaned heavily on the popular Disney effect, combined with a contemporary Broadway feeling. In 1966, it was proposed to build a Washington Irving Amphitheater not far from the site of Rip's Retreat, and there, present through each summer, a musical show based on the story of Rip. The site was spectacular; the show's script and music were approved by eminent drama critic Brooks Atkinson, and a vigorous campaign was launched to raise the needed capital. The amphitheater was planned to seat 3,000, with buildings in a Dutch style to house shops, a restaurant, and space in which patrons might take shelter in case of rain. After a hard struggle by its promoters, the project was dropped when not enough money could be raised.

Since the failure of the amphitheater plan, Rip Van Winkle's sleep has grown even deeper. Since then, much as been printed about the Catskills—the voluminous, statistic-studded reports of a New York State Commission to Study the Catskills, and reports on many aspects of the region by private promotional, conservation, and other organizations. In all these, Rip is not mentioned. He seems no longer to be seen as having any relation to the Catskills. The guardian spirit of the Catskills has disappeared, and with him has gone the stir of the imagination to which the very name of the Catskills once gave rise.

The most ambitious of all attempts at staging an annual performance of the Rip play in the Catskills was planned in 1966-68 in a musical version by Kermit Goell. The open-air theater shown here was to be located high on the mountainside not far from what was thought to be the sight of Rip's adventure.   FROM A PROMOTIONAL BOOKLET, 1966-68, AUTHOR'S COLLECTION

Will Rip Van Winkle ever awaken and return to his place as the guardian spirit of the Catskills? That cannot be ruled out, for in recent years there has been much evidence to show that an awakening of the imagination of Americans is underway. Books on gnomes and fairies have become bestsellers; science and space fantasy and for many the revival of ancient religious cults and of witchcraft are lightening the burden of a mechanized society.

Rip Van Winkle might someday awaken with delight and energy into this new world and remake the Catskills into the enchanted region it once was.

Aeronaut John Wise as shown in the frontispiece of his
A System of Aeronautics, *Philadelpha, 1850.*

WHOSE BALLOON
IS IT?

NINETEEN EIGHTY-THREE WAS WIDELY CELEBRA-
ted as the two-hundredth anniversary of
the first balloon ascension—this event took
place in France. In 1793, George Washington witnessed the first American ascen-
sion, and ever since balloons have been part of American life.

During the nineteenth century, balloon ascen-
sions in the Catskills were often features of county
fairs, Fourth of July celebrations, and entertainments
for summer boarders. No ascension in the Catskills has
left any significant mark on the history of the development of ballooning. Yet if you search the index of
almost any book about the history of human adventures in the air, you are likely to find one reference to
the Catskills.

If you follow this clue, it will lead you to an account
of an immensely publicized attempt at a transatlantic
crossing in 1873. It was sponsored by the owners of the
New York Daily Graphic and came to a very premature

end in North Canaan in the northwestern corner of Connecticut. This unfortunate landing is mistakenly placed in the Catskills.

In trying to track down the route by which this error found its way into so many respected books, I was led, little by little, into the story of the relationship of the Catskill Mountains and balloons. I found that this story dealt with the role of the Catskills as a balloon-catcher—a role for which the mountains are eminently qualified by their height above the surrounding country and their sometimes sudden changes of wind and weather.

The Catskills caught their first balloon on May 4, 1844. This balloon belonged to the same John Wise who would later originate the *Daily Graphic's* venture of 1873.

During the afternoon of May 4, 1844, Wise, an able aeronaut (so balloonists were called at the time), was inflating his new balloon, the *Vesperus*, in preparation for an ascent at Hallidaysburg, Pennsylvania. The balloon was a new and experimental one made of tussah silk, a light brown fabric originating in the cocoons of wild moths of India and China.

In those days before federal weather reports were available, an aeronaut had to rely on his own weather judgment. Wise was confident that the strong wind then blowing would allow a safe take-off. However, the wind grew so violent that the *Vesperus* tugged and rolled as it was being filled with hydrogen gas. Finally it was filled, and at once rose to a great height. It was caught by a powerful wind from the southwest and aimed directly at a threatening mass of black clouds to the northeast.

Wise became worried. He released gas in order to cause the *Vesperus* to sink beneath the clouds. The balloon sank obediently but almost to the ground. Wise threw out his anchor, or grapnel. With the anchor tearing up bushes and fences, the balloon bounded along until it became tangled in the top of a tall tree. Wise tried to free the *Vesperus*—and in the attempt stepped out of its car into the ropes that held the gas bag and car together. A gust of wind turned him upside down; with his teeth, Wise held open the gas valve. One of his feet became snarled in the ropes. Then another gust separated Wise and the balloon. The balloon shot up and raced toward the Catskills.

That evening, while he nursed his cuts and bruises, Wise gave an account of the day's adventures to a reporter for a local newspaper, the *Register*. The *Register* got out an extra devoted to Wise's story and sent it out to other papers in several states. The *Register* said that Wise doubted that he'd ever see his balloon again, but thanks to its newspaper coverage, Wise eventually would have a reunion with the *Vesperus*.

The *Catskill Recorder* helped bring aeronaut and balloon together again when it printed a story headed "Whose Balloon Is It?" The paper told of the landing of a mysterious balloon in the Greene County town of Lexington.

Among the newspapers that received both *Register* and *Recorder* stories were the *Albany Argus* and the *New York Tribune*. Both papers quoted the *Recorder* as stating,

on the evening of the 4th inst. a balloon lighted on the premises of the Rev. John P. Van Valkenburgh of Lexington in this county. The car which was attached to the balloon contained a lady's basket in which was a quantity of cake, a small bottle, a tin cup and several papers printed at Hallidaysburg, Pa. and dated May 4. Attached to the basket was a paper on which was written, 'John Wise, Philadelphia.'

Word of the finding of the *Vesperus* was slow in getting to Wise. How he found it later in May he described in his *System of Aeronautics*, published in Philadelphia in 1850:

> Mr. Van Valkenburgh's son was out in the field ploughing round the hemlock stumps [Lexington was just ending its tannery period and was pock-marked with stumps] when the balloon was coming down and upon seeing it in the air thought it was an immense bird of prey pouncing down upon him, which alarmed him to such a degree that after he had fled to the house he was affected with violent spasms. The balloon was suffered to roll and toss about the hemlock stumps before it was secured.

Lexington people, Wise wrote, were baffled at finding Hallidaysburg newspapers dated that very day in the balloon's car. They had never heard of the place, and when they looked it up "in their geographies," they learned with astonishment that it lay "hundreds of miles to the southwest over the mountains and rivers."

By the time Wise arrived, his balloon had been cut into six pieces by people bent on salvaging the silk. Wise informed local people about balloons so effectively that they begged him to return and make an ascension for them—but this he never did. He sent the parts of the balloon back to Pennsylvania, assembled them and made several flights in the re-constituted *Vesperus*.

Every now and then, an early aeronaut floated above the Catskills and managed to avoid being caught in the arms of mountaintop trees or marooned in clearings. One lucky aeronaut was Washington Donaldson. He had been in command of the *Daily Graphic* venture after its originator, John Wise, had backed out in disgust at the blatant publicity and slipshod craftsmanship that marred the attempt. Favorable winds carried Donaldson and a party of newspaper reporters from New York up the Hudson Valley to Columbia County, where balloon and passengers spent the night. The next morning, the balloon floated all on board across the Catskills and came down near Saratoga. The trip was not lacking in bad moments. Said the *New York Times*, "Professor Donaldson [by then this title was given to all American aeronauts] had some narrow escapes from catching in the pines over the Catskills."

In 1883, a less-fortunate balloon didn't manage to elude the treetops of the Catskills. Then, Professor Grinley was making what promised to be a routine ascension on the Fourth of July from Honesdale, Pennsylvania. A storm developed suddenly, and a powerful wind carried balloon and professor at a high speed toward the northeast.

"The great Slide Mountain advanced toward me," Grinley recalled. "I was horrified at seeing a terrific storm gathering on Slide's summit. The mountaintop seemed 'aflame' with lightning." Peals of thunder assaulted Grinley's ears and nerves. He realized that he was "hemmed in between two storms." The balloon's car struck the top of a tree, and the winds tried in vain to tear it loose. As rain and wind continued, Grinley abandoned the balloon and wriggled and fell down the tree.

After wandering in some confusion, he climbed a tree and caught a glimpse of an inhabited house. He found his way there through the storm—it was the house of "Andrew J. Mabie near Revilo Mulenix' sawmill," said the *Kingston Daily Freeman* in a story headed "Perils of Ballooning." Grinley spent the night at Mabie's and the next morning rounded up a group of local men who helped him unsnarl the balloon and get it down to the Big Indian railroad station.

Grinley's misadventures did nothing to check other balloonists from making ascents of a more normal sort within and around the Catskills. Professor Van Devere, for one, made a "beautiful ascension" from the Margaretville Fair Grounds in 1889. A patriotic ascension was made as part of the Bicentennial Celebration in 1976 in Woodstock. A hot-air balloon of about 60 feet in height rose to about 400 feet in the almost-windless air and then drifted to a relaxed landing on the nearby golf course. This balloon owed its hot air to a propane burner. Similar burners are used by modern followers of a new wave of interest in ballooning as a sport.

With improved weather forecasting, better materials for making balloons, and propane burners, which give a greater degree of control than anything available to the balloonists of Wise's day, the Catskills' role as a balloon-catcher has diminished. Yet the statement that the spectacular transatlantic *Daily Graphic* balloon came to grief in the Catskills goes on turning up in print, and gives the Catskills an unearned but apparently secure niche in the story of American ballooning.

The aborted balloon flight of 1873 across the Atlantic stimulated Joseph Walz as he awaited hanging in the Catskill jail to draw the balloon as he imagined it floating above his family farm.

COURTESY OF THE GREENE COUNTY HISTORICAL SOCIETY

Portrait of Henry Rowe Schoolcraft, 1793-1864. He was a voluminous writer on Indians and the inventor of the name "Onteora."

FROM AN ENGRAVING IN E.A. AND G.L. DUYCKINCK, CYCLOPEDIA OF AMERICAN LITERATURE, NEW YORK, 1853

CHANGE THE NAME OF THE CATSKILLS? HELL NO!

DURING THE CHILLY DAYS AND NIGHTS OF WINTER, a recent revival of an old movement has been making some underground headway among the Catksills. In places where young people gather to eat, drink, or dance, there has been discussion of changing the name of the Catskills. The movement has surfaced here and there and has been commented on in at least one regional newspaper. What the backers of the movement would like to do is to change the name of the Catskills to Onteora.

In many parts of this turbulent world, old names are being thrown out and new ones that express freedom from oppression and colonialism are being substituted. So *Basutoland* has become *Lesotho*, and *Congo* has become *Zaire*. It is not surprising that Americans who are organized to do justice to the long-oppressed American Indians, or Native Americans, should think of expressing their aims by a return to what they believe to be Indian place names. But here in the Catskills, a change like this would meet serious difficulties. For one thing, the present name of the region has so deeply entrenched itself in the affections of the people that it has survived all former campaigns to change it.

The name by which we know our mountains was given over three centuries ago by the Dutch invaders who pushed the Indians out of the Hudson Valley and imposed their own culture on the region. The exact origin of the name *Catskills* is obscure, and at present only conjectures are possible. By 1664, the name was under fire for the first time. That year, the British displaced the Dutch as rulers of the Province of New York and launched a drive to root out Dutch ways. Then *New Amsterdam* became *New York*, *Fort Orange* became *Albany* and the *Nieuw Dorp* became *Hurley*.

To British ears, the name Catskills sounded too Dutch to be worth preserving, and so a steady drive was begun to force the change of the name to the *Blue Mountains*. The new name made some headway among lawyers and officials, but the people of the region resisted it as stubbornly as they resisted the accompanying attempts to change their daily language and their religious denominations.

The Livingstons, of Clermont-on-the-Hudson, had no better luck when they tried in the mid-eighteenth century to change the name of the Catskills to the *Lothian Hills*—this to honor their Scottish ancestors and the mountains familiar to them.

After the Indians had receded from a position of power in the Hudson Valley and the Catskills, they lost, in many white minds, the image of a hostile people fit only to be exterminated. They acquired instead the feeling of the romantic, natural people given form and currency as the "noble savages" of Jean Jacques Rousseau. Here and there, as the nineteenth century was born and began to grow, voices were raised to advocate honoring the Indians by restoring to the Catskills their "old Indian name." However, an insuperable obstacle seemed to arise—there was no old Indian name for the Catskills.

The Algonkian-speaking Indians who had used the Catskills as hunting grounds lived in a culture that differed in many ways from that of their white conquerors. For example, they did not use the kind of place names that Europeans imposed on every river, lake, valley, and settlement. A river like the Hudson might be known to the Indians by many names, each applying to one point in the river's course and none capable of being applied to the river as a whole. The same was true of mountain ranges like the Catskills.

The demand for an Indian name for the Catskills grew as romanticism expanded under the influence of poets and novelists. In 1843, Indian expert Henry Rowe Schoolcraft put together just the name that was wanted. He joined two Iroquoian roots for the words meaning "mountain" and "sky" and so invented *Onteora*. (Schoolcraft was skillful at this kind of name-making. In 1832, he had put together two Latin syllables plus the letter "i" to form a new name for a midwestern lake. The lake had been called *Omushkos*, which meant "Elk Lake." This Schoolcraft changed to *Itasca*, which sounded very pretty and very "Indian" to most American ears.)

In neither case did Schoolcraft intend to fool anyone; he made it plain that he was inventing names that he believed to be more suitable than the old ones. But as years passed by, Schoolcraft's explanations were forgotten. *Onteora, Onti-Ora,* or other variants became accepted as genuine Indian names. A large body of "lore" and "legend" arose. Kingston poet Henry Abbey wrote of a giant named Onteora whose bones became the rocks of the Catskills and whose eyes became North and South Lakes. Some of the Indian lore reported by Washington Irving in a note to his tale of Rip Van Winkle was worked into the Onteora story. Guide books and advertisers for booming Catskill Mountain summer resorts welcomed Onteora with enthusiasm, and a residential park and club and a Hudson River steamboat were named Onteora. Schoolcraft's explanation of the name as meaning "mountain joined to sky" became "Land of the Sky," because this form was felt to sound more euphonious and more Indian.

It is unlikely that the movement to change the name of the Catskills will get very far. Such movements seldom do, for our attachment to familiar place names is very strong. A good example of the emotions that place-name tinkering can arouse came along about a century ago when it was proposed to change the spelling and pronunciation of the name of *Arkansas.* Then, it is said, a member of the state legislature stood up and launched into an impassioned oration that has become a classic of American folklore—its theme was "Change the name of Arkansas? Hell, no!" Should the proposal to change the name of the Catskills gain ground, it is likely that a similar war cry will echo among our mountains.

Onteora is a very pretty name and anyone who wants to use it has every right to do so. But it can be best used as a tribute to the white people who first showed appreciation and understanding of the American Indian and tried, however mistakenly, to express their feelings in a word.

The part that the Indians have played in life on this continent deserves to be honored, and a simple sense of justice and respect for human rights makes it appropriate that we recognize what we owe to the Indians. At this time, when we realize the extent that our natural resources have been squandered, we might well take some action, here among the Catskills, to direct attention toward the respect for the natural world that had so large a place in Indian culture and to their way of living in harmony with their environment. Changing the name of the Catskills to one invented by a white man would not accomplish this.

Instead, we might try to learn more about the way the Indians lived on their Catskill Mountain hunting grounds. We can still study some of the rock shelters used for many centuries by Indian hunters; one of these might be preserved from the destruction that awaits and become the center of an attempt at honoring our Indian predecessors and learning from them something of their earth wisdom.

*Photograph of Ned Buntline, c. 1890, showing
him wearing his dubious decorations.*

THE LIFE AND ADVENTURES
OF NED BUNTLINE

T HE CATSKILLS, LIKE OTHER MOUNTAIN REGIONS, have produced a good many of the kind of people sometimes called "oddballs"—people who do not conform to standards of behavior customary in their society. It is likely that the oddest—and the most famous—of all Catskill Mountain oddballs was Edward Zane Carroll Judson, better known to the readers of his time by his pen name, Ned Buntline.*

The people of Stamford in the northern Catskills, where Ned was born in 1823, still debate whether they should feel proud or ashamed of Ned. He changed the reading habits of Americans and played a key part in creating the myth of the American West. But he also shot people in and out of duels, served time in prison, indulged in bigamy, and played the part of a racist rabble-rouser.

The Stamford of the time of Ned's arrival in the Catskills served as an appropriate beginning for his

*A *buntline* is a rope used to haul up a sail for furling.

flamboyant career. It had been settled before the Revolution, abandoned during the war, and resettled when the war was over. A busy turnpike passed through the town, and the rowdiness of turnpike teamsters and drovers at local taverns gave the place the nickname of "the Devil's Half Acre."

When Ned was a young child, his family moved to Pennsylvania where his writing, orating, and teaching father saw a bright future. But that future darkened, and Ned became a runaway on board a merchant ship bound for the tropics from Philadelphia. After several years at sea, short, broad, and red-haired Ned took part as a U.S. Navy man in the Seminole War in Florida. While still in his teens he acquired the reputation of a fast man with a gun and a skillful and daring horseman.

By 1842, Ned was putting to practical use his already varied experiences. He edited magazines: one was called, in reference to Ned's tales of life at sea, *Ned Buntline's Magazine*. It later became popular as *Ned Buntline's Own*. Before long, Ned was turning out the first of the many cheaply printed thrillers he would write. Titles of early ones were *Magdelena, The Beautiful Mexican Maid*, and *The Black Avenger of the Spanish Main; or the Fiend of Blood*.

After escaping a Nashville, Tennessee, lynching mob set on avenging his killing a man in a duel, Ned made for New York. There he ground out further shockers, including one dealing with life in the city's slums—it was called *The Mysteries and Miseries of New York*. Although he was himself a heavy drinker, Ned appeared before the public as a temperance lecturer.

He joined the nativist agitation of the day, which was directed against Irish and German Roman Catholic immigrants. He led a mob of anti-Britishers in what was known as the Astor Place Riot, in which twenty-two people were killed. For this Ned served a year in prison.

Even in prison, Ned went on writing. His novelettes were the first of the kind that would soon become known as "dime novels." They all dealt in a lurid way with past and present American life.

Following his release from prison in New York (to the cheers of his nativist followers), Ned traveled in the South and West, giving temperance lectures and agitating against newly arrived immigrants. He led a riot directed against Catholic Germans in St. Louis and successfully fled from the law. After a while, he took to living in an isolated cabin in the Adirondacks with a local girl as his mate. He named the cabin the "Eagle's Nest." During these years, Ned ceaselessly ground out his thrillers and saw them advance in popularity and profitability. At the Eagle's Nest he perfected his skill in fishing, hunting, and woodcraft.

When the Civil War came, Ned enlisted as a private. His abilities brought him quickly to the rank of sergeant. Despite punishment after a spell of drinking, he left the army with an honorable discharge. Ever afterwards, Ned claimed to have served as a colonel of scouts during the war.

The Civil War may not have made Ned a colonel, but it certainly boosted the popularity of the kind of fiction he wrote. Dime novels had an enormous attraction to soldiers who read them during the slack periods of their army life. These books led to the pulp magazines of later times and, in a roundabout way, to the paperback publishing industry of today.

After the war, Ned turned his attention to Western subjects. In 1869, he went to Nebraska to interview an Indian fighter whom he hoped to make the hero of a series of tales. The fighter refused to cooperate; instead, Ned talked with a handsome young man named William Cody. He wrote a magazine serial about Cody, whom he named Buffalo Bill. The story was called *Buffalo Bill; the King of the Border Men-The Wildest and Truest Story I Ever Wrote*. Most of the incidents in the story were news to Cody. A play about Buffalo Bill followed, and then, with Cody as star, the world's first Wild West Show with Ned as director and an actor.

The death of his uncle, Samuel Judson, brought Ned back to his native Stamford. There, he took steps toward planning the library that his uncle had bequeathed to the town. Wearing moccasins and fringed buckskin pants, Ned pitched an elaborate tent and demonstrated his marksmanship with gusto—using inanimate targets. He decided to make Stamford his home base.

Soon, he was busy building an elegant country house which he again named Eagle's Nest; he married a local woman and settled down as a part-time resident, active in local affairs and, at first, respected for his evidence of wealth, his national fame, and his geniality toward his neighbors. On the Fourth of July, he entertained Stamford with a splendid display of fireworks. He read poems of his own writing on local occasions. And, on special occasions, he would wear a dark blue coat, which suggested a military origin, with a display of miscellaneous medals on his chest. Altogether, Colonel Judson, as he was called, seemed a very solid and substantial citizen. It was true that tales of the colonel's early misdeeds surfaced now and then, but he always explained them away.

The Stamford of Ned's years at the Eagle's Nest was no longer called the Devil's Half Acre; it was emerging as a well-kept and respectable summer resort where Ned's lecture on the evils of alcohol was well received. The Eagle's Nest, with its conservatory, gun and trophy room, library, and rolling lawns, was a local showplace. The large income Ned earned by his writing made Stamford people regard him with a kind of awe. It was not until a woman claiming to be his true wife turned up that many Stamford people grew cool toward Ned. Ned did his best to explain away the lady and continued to play the role of a prosperous and respected country gentleman.

By the 1880s, Ned was showing the effects of his hard life and years. His gait was a bit unsteady, and he was troubled by the many wounds that he still liked to display to callers while giving varied accounts of their origins. As he grew older, Ned lavished love and attention on his final batch of children. When his daughter Irene died, Ned had a white marble statue of an angel placed on her grave. The death of the last of his children, a little son on whom Ned came to center all his hopes, left him shattered. He died, after a difficult last few years, in 1886.

Time has clouded but not eliminated Stamford's remembrance of its renowned author. For a century,

"Eagle's Nest" was and remains a Stamford showplace.   AUTHOR'S PHOTOGRAPH

Stamford girls have placed an occasional bouquet of flowers on Irene's grave. The little girl angel has now lost her wings and become dark and discolored. A few feet from her is Ned's grave decorated with an American flag in tribute to his military career—he is named Colonel E. Z. C. Judson on the obelisk, which rises over his family plot. The Eagle's Nest remains outwardly much as it was in Ned's time. The Stamford Library has some Buntline memorabilia—plates decorated with a picture of an eagle's nest, a cane with a goldplated head given to Ned by Buffalo Bill, and so on.

A biography of Ned entitled *The Great Rascal: The Life and Adventures of Ned Buntline* was published in 1951 by Jay Monaghan. Monaghan's judgment of Ned is perhaps overly harsh, given the confusion into which his life story has been thrown (in part by Ned's own obfuscations). It might be well to display a little charity toward him and suggest that the exciting mixture of fact and fancy that marked his stories somehow spilled over into his own existence and turned Ned's life into his own best dime novel.

Left to right on an Onteora verandah, summer of 1890: Mark Twain, painter Carroll Beckwith, and Laurence Hutton and Brander Mathews who were eminent literary critics of the day.

MARK TWAIN AS AN ONTEORIAN—1890

LMOST EVERY ACCOUNT OF SUMMER LIFE IN the Catskills during the nineteenth century makes much of the visits of such celebrities as Presidents U.S. Grant and Chester A. Arthur, Civil War General William T. Sherman, Senator Daniel Webster, poet and editor William Cullen Bryant, and painter Thomas Cole. All had one thing in common: these heroes either stayed at one of the region's great commercial summer hotels or glorified them in words or paint.

The hotel managers were keenly aware of the value of big names in attracting paying guests. They furnished free room and board to newspapermen in return for stories featuring illustrious guests, whom the managers had often lured to their establishments by ingenious means. All of this made good sense as far as the big hotels were concerned, but after 1880 a new kind of resort appeared in the region whose managers did things differently. These were the private enclaves known as "parks."

While the hotels advertised with frantic energy, the parks did not. They courted obscurity and seemed to do their best to keep the public from crossing their boundaries. There was a persuasive reason for this apparent bashfulness, a reason that grew out of the very nature of the parks. The parks were usually founded by people whose parents and grandparents had enjoyed the kind of summer life that flourished at the Catskill Mountain House between its beginnings in 1823 and the decline that set in during the 1870s. The enjoyment of natural scenery, of a romantic involvement with nature, of the arts, and of vigorous outdoor activity were all highly valued by the white, Anglo-Saxon, Protestant park people. They established their parks as places to which they might retreat—away from the commercial hotels to which newer Americans, whom they considered to be of lesser social standing or of different ways (especially the Roman Catholics and the Jews) were thronging (and to which these new-comers were adding elements of their own cultures). Because the parks were owned by private organizations, they had the right, under law, to choose their members and guests.

One notable guest chosen by Onteora Park was author, lecturer and humorist Samuel L. Clemens, known on both sides of the Atlantic under the pen name of Mark Twain. Together with his wife and daughters, he spent the summer of 1890 at Onteora Park. Not only did the whole family delight the Onteoreans, but the visit shed light for our benefit on the great author's complex personality and on the character of the park.

Mark Twain's early conditioning had been very different from that of most park people. He came from the small Mississippi River town of Hannibal, Missouri, whose culture he had absorbed. Contact with the wider world, especially after his marriage to Olivia Langdon, who shared in many of the park people's values, enabled him to slip easily into the park environment.

It was at the invitation of Candace Wheeler that Mark Twain came to Onteora Park. Mrs. Wheeler's strong character dominated the park, which she and her brother, prosperous wholesale grocer Francis Thurber, had founded in 1883. From a start in life as the daughter of a Delhi, New York, storekeeper, Candace had gone on to become one of the leaders of the aesthetic movement of the 1870s, an associate of Louis Comfort Tiffany (of Tiffany glass fame) and of Lockwood De Forest.

As a designer of textiles, wallpaper, and interiors, Mrs. Wheeler left her mark on the taste of her time. Among the projects on which she worked with Tiffany and De Forest was the redecoration in 1883 of the house in Hartford, Connecticut, built by Mark Twain in 1874. The house, now owned by the Mark Twain Memorial Association, is an extraordinary one in its profusion of turrets and verandahs, its varied textures, its stenciled wall coverings, its colored glass, and furniture in which traditional ideas are given fresh turns.

When Mark Twain arrived at Onteora Park, he stood at the summit of his career. *Tom Sawyer, Huckleberry Finn, The Innocents Abroad, Roughing It*, and his popular lectures had made him both rich and famous.

His tremendous energy, his story-telling talent, and his gift for striking and amusing conversation had made him a hero to presidents and kings, financiers, society leaders, and literary dictators. And he reveled in being accepted as one of the very greatest celebrities of his time. An obsessive yearning for business success had led him to involvement in publishing and into backing the inventor of a typesetting machine that he hoped would make obsolete the kind of drudgery he himself had once endured as a young Western printer. These projects would, before long, lead Mark Twain into bankruptcy, but as he reached Onteora the storm had not yet gathered.

It was Mark Twain's firm intention to work steadily at Onteora on a sequel to two of his best books, to be called *Tom Sawyer and Huckleberry Finn Among the Indians*. But the book went badly and ground to a halt—it was never finished. Yet, if his Onteora summer was a failure as a working vacation, it was an immense social success. For Mark Twain and his family charmed Onteoreans as they had never been charmed before. The great author was available on friendly terms to everyone in the park, and he had everyone chuckling at his witty talk. He and his daughters staged dramatic entertainments, both impromptu and carefully planned. Because the family was planning to go to Europe, the girls were studying German, and this gave rise to a farce in which a chorus chanted the conjugation of the verb *Haben* throughout the performance.

Mark Twain was famous for his skill in reading aloud, and he read in the evening to Onteoreans seated on a grassy slope. He was the star attraction at dinner parties, where his flashing wit charmed the resident celebrities, who were many. Mary Mapes Dodge was one—she was editor of *St. Nicholas* magazine, to which the country's most eminent writers were proud to contribute. Laurence Hutton was another—he was a drama and literary critic, a friend of the great of the world of books and a prolific author of biography and criticism. Brander Matthews was another Onteorean—he was a professor of English at Columbia University whose authoritative views on literature were widely accepted.

There were more—people who had secure reputations in theater, music, and painting. The leading painter was James Carroll Beckwith, who like Mark Twain came from Hannibal, Missouri. Beckwith was a very successful genre and portrait painter. He taught by summer in the studio he had built at Onteora and there painted such subjects as *A Baptism at Onteora* and *The Blacksmith*. Beckwith set about painting a portrait of Mark Twain that shows the author at the very peak of his vigorous and charismatic prime—and the painter at his best, as well.

And as if it were not enough to exert his power to please adult Onteoreans, Mark Twain was long-remembered by the children with whom he romped and played, turning ordinary little games into memorable occasions.

Mark Twain often described himself as lazy. It may be that he found the pleasures of being a celebrity so entrancing that they sometimes kept him from his work. At Onteora, he wrote nothing that could place him beside Irving, Bryant, or Cooper as an interpreter of the Catskills; in fact, he is not generally known to have written anything at all in the park but a single letter. That letter, which was never sent and remained unknown until its publication after Twain's death in 1910, contains an important insight into Samuel Clemens, the person behind the author, lecturer, and humorist.

The editor of an anti-czarist magazine, *Free Russia*, had asked Twain to comment on efforts being made by Russian dissidents to throw off the tyranny of the czars. A series of articles by George Kennan, then appearing in the magazine *The Outlook*, was harrowing Americans with its revelations of the cruel oppression of the Russian people by their czar. In his unsent reply, Twain said that he felt the liberation efforts being made were far too mild. He stated that so monstrous a tyranny as that of the czar should never be overthrown without bloodshed and that "my privilege to write these sanguinary sentences in soft security was bought for me by rivers of blood poured out upon many fields, in many lands but I possess not one single little paltry right or privilege that comes to me as a result of petition, persuasion, agitation for reform or any kindred method of procedure. . . ." He went on to advocate assassination of the Russian rulers.

In recent years, Hal Holbrook, in his *Mark Twain Tonight*, has given the public a better understanding of a side of Mark Twain that was often ignored or even suppressed during his lifetime. This was the side in which his sardonic view of the human race and his gift for black humor flourished. His letter to the editor of *Free Russia* forcibly expresses the dark, pessimistic aspect of his nature.

Those of us who love the Catskills will always regret that while Mark Twain so thoroughly enjoyed the "soft security" of Onteora Park he did not write something that might have placed him among the great writers whose imaginations have been aroused by the Catskills. We shall have to make do with the unsent letter that shows us that deep emotions sometimes seethed beneath the placid and civilized surface of life at Onteora Park in the year 1890.

The steam launch Wawaka afloat on Halcottsville Lake with its skipper and maker Burr Hubbell looking out from the wheelhouse, around 1903. COURTESY OF GUY GRAYBILL

STEAMBOATING AMONG
THE CATSKILLS

THE STORY OF STEAM-POWERED RAILROAD EN-
gines puffing their way through the Catskills has often been told and has roused a
nostalgia, culminating now and then in
proposals to revive the old Ulster and Delaware Railroad. Less familiar and less important—yet
with a considerable interest of their own—are other
regional uses of steam, which was the original motive
power of the Ulster and Delaware. For example, there
is the case of Burr Hubbell, who once designed, made,
and operated a steamboat on an artificial lake on the
East Branch of the Delaware River.

It was the pioneer railroads of the 1830s that introduced the power of steam to the Catskills. By 1865,
according to the New York State Census, steam was
beginning to take the place of the waterpower that had
long been among the Catskills' most valued resources.
A century earlier, as Scotland's James Watt was working his way toward designing a practicable steam engine, water-powered sawmills had begun converting

the logs that resulted from clearing the land into lumber that was floated down the nearby Hudson and Delaware rivers to market. During the first half of the nineteenth century, the abundant waterpower of the Catskills was put to work making yarn, cloth, leather, barrels, and a great variety of wooden objects. Once dams, flumes, waterwheels, pulleys, and belts were in place, a water-powered mill might go on for years with no cost for energy—barring floods, which damaged or swept away an occasional mill.

Despite its economy, waterpower had some drawbacks. When the flow of streams dwindled in late summer, so too did their flow of power, and often work had to be suspended. An old way of hazing an innocent boy, newly come to work during a dry spell, was to order him to go upstream and spit in the creek in order to increase its flow. In hard winters, ice sometimes formed on waterwheels and impeded their turning.

For years, these were petty annoyances. But as American industry became ever more tightly organized and a year-round, ten-hour-a-day, six-day-a-week schedule became normal, water-powered mills found it hard to meet the competition of those using steam. Then, some watermills in the Catskills installed steam engines to take over when waterpower failed, and steam-powered sawmills proliferated. Wood-using industries like furniture factories and turning shops, as well as sawmills, fueled their steam engines with scrap wood and so needed no cash outlay for fuel. As the nineteenth century neared its end, steam was gaining on waterpower. The machinery on display in the Hanford Mills Museum at East Meredith well documents this process.

It was only a matter of time in a steam-conscious world before a steamboat would appear on some body of water among the Catskills. In 1885, George Harding, owner and builder of the Catskills' most elegant hotel, the Kaaterskill, bought a ready-made little steamboat to be used on South Lake, which then formed part of Harding's hotel park. Six teams of horses hauled the boat up the mountain from the Hudson River at Catskill to the cheers and wonder of crowds. The boat was named the *Gussie Paige*, in honor of the Kaaterskill's manager's daughter, and treated capacity loads of sixteen summer people to rides around the lake.

Soon, wherever ponds or lakes could be found in the Catskills, hosts of summer boarders were examining them and wondering if a steamboat might not become an added attraction for summer guests.

In 1883, Burr Hubbell and his brother Wallace had begun dealing in farm machinery, coal, grain, and lumber. (Hubbell Brothers were long in business near Margaretville.) The pair were inventive. As bicycling became popular, the Hubbells designed, manufactured, and marketed a bicycle of their own. By 1898, a steamboat was afloat on Halcottsville Pond, newly renamed Lake Wawaka. The boat named the *Wawaka*, had been designed and built by Burr, who also served as the boat's master as he guided it around the lake with its summer passengers. Each summer for ten years Burr captained and crewed the *Wawaka*, until 1908, when he sold it to Charles C. Vermilyea, who had just vanquished many difficulties and completed Lake Switzerland in Fleischmanns. For two seasons the *Wawaka* went round and round the new lake, its American flag fluttering and smoke trailing from its mini-smokestack.

By 1910, the internal combustion engine powered by gasoline had proved its value in small boat use. The *Wawaka* gave way to a new motorboat and slowly fell apart. The engine that Burr Hubbell had made was salvaged and returned to its birthplace in Halcottsville. There it remained in the keeping of Wallace Hubbell's descendants (Burr had no children) until not many years ago, when it was sold to be displayed in an upstate museum.

The water impounded as Lake Wawaka has served the people of the vicinity in many ways — as the power source of a fulling mill, a grist mill, and for a short time, of a small hydroelectric project that supplied the hamlet of Halcottsville. The lake was put to use too as a recreational spot for the summer boarders attracted by the rural charm of the valley — the boarders danced by night on a lantern-lit raft afloat on the lake. It was also used by winter as a source of ice. The ice was shipped to Kingston via the Ulster and Delaware Railroad, the tracks of which skirt the lake. And every day, ice was taken from a lakeside icehouse to be used in cooling cans of local milk as they traveled by rail to the city of New York. All this is a matter of pride to old Halcottsville people. But they are proudest of their own Burr Hubbell, the steamboat man.

Placid Halcottsville Lake as shown on page 78 in the 1903 edition of the Ulster & Delaware's The Catskill Mountains. The Most Picturesque Mountain Region on the Globe.

In this 1849 painting by Asher B. Durand, Thomas Cole and poet William Cullen Bryant, two friends and lovers of the Catskills are shown admiring an idealized version of the famous Catskill Cloves.

CATSKILL CLOVES AND
CATSKILL PAINTERS

SOME ZEALOUS LOVERS OF THE CATSKILLS HAVE expressed annoyance with the term "Hudson River School" of landscape painters. They have pointed out that the men of this school first worked in the Catskill Mountains and so might properly be said to belong to a "Catskill Mountain School." And it would be possible for an enthusiast for the Catskills' charms to go even farther and group Thomas Cole, Asher B. Durand, Thomas Doughty, John F. Kensett, and the other nineteenth-century painters of the Catskills as the "Clove Painters." For these men owed much of their early reputations to their paintings of the streams, the rocks, and especially the waterfalls of what were often referred to as "The Cloves of the Catskills."

Just what is a "clove"? In the broad sense in which the word was used by seventeenth-century settlers of New Netherlands, it meant a pass or notch between two hills or mountains. In the special sense it came to have in the Catskills, it most often meant a narrow, precipitous gorge down which a stream plunged in a series of falls and rapids.

When a mid-nineteenth-century Catskill Mountain summer hotel owner advertised that his place was convenient to "the Cloves," he was referring to the Kaaterskill and Plattekill Cloves, with the Stony Clove sometimes included. The Kaaterskill and Plattekill Cloves are the results of breaks in the great eastern wall of the Catskills, to which nineteenth-century romantics gave the pseudo-Indian name of the "Wall of Manitou." The Stony Clove, some miles westward of the brink of the Wall, is milder and contains not a rushing stream but a brooding pond. This clove and its pond were formed when impounded waters burst through a mountain barrier as the last Ice Age ended. The other two cloves, with the help of a slight tilting of the bedrock, resulted from a relentless process of erosion of weaker strata of the Catskills' layered rocks and the tumbling down of stronger ones immediately above.

The Kaaterskill and Plattekill Cloves, wrote Henry E. Dwight in the *American Journal of Science* in 1819, exhibit "the bold bluff, the tremendous precipice, and the awful chasm which so strongly mark the sublime." All this should suggest that when Thomas Cole, the earliest member of the Hudson River School, arrived in the Catskills in 1825, he found the landscape, and especially the cloves, well prepared for his purpose.

The preparation, of course, had begun much further back in the human past. Clefts in rocky cliffs have stirred human emotions as far back as we can see among people of many and varied cultures. Beliefs that human and animal ancestors first emerged from within

Mother Earth through clefts in the rocks are widely distributed. In the thirteenth century, St. Odilo is said to have come upon a cleft in a cliff and looked into it to see the fires of Purgatory, and so was inspired to initiate All Souls Day. We need not be reminded of the use of caves and rock clefts as human dwellings, as burial places, as temples and shrines, and as sites for the earliest-known wall paintings. Modern psychologists have found caves and clefts to be powerful sexual symbols.

In eighteenth-century Europe, the rise of romantic feeling drew marked attention to clefts and caves. Artificial caves called *grottoes* were created to enhance landscape designs. Waterfalls became objects of pilgrimage by the aesthetically aware. The horror once aroused by gloomy mountain passes with "impending rocks" and "dashing cataracts" was transformed to pleasure. By the second half of the eighteenth century, the new fashion for seeing the landscape was being enjoyed by travelers on the Hudson. But the character of the Catskills' major cloves was invisible from the River.

Early explorers and surveyors within the Catskills paid little attention to the cloves. They climbed the eastern wall of the mountains by zig-zagging up their rock-terraced slopes rather than struggling with the confusion of the two principal cloves that break the wall—the Kaaterskill and the Plattekill.

The reason for ignoring the cloves as means of access to the heights was made clear by Peter De Labigarre, who climbed Overlook Mountain in April 1793 and returned to the Hudson Valley by means of the Plattekill Clove, which he found to be "the most arduous (route) I could meet with." First of all travelers in the region who left behind a record of their impressions in print, De Labigarre saw the clove in romantic terms. He found the mountain at the foot of the great waterfall high in the clove "to be split asunder as if to let the bold traveler look into its bowels. On the south side of that stupendous gap, the top being crowned with a thick row of evergreen, never permitted the rays of the sun to approach that cold and horrid place." A little later that same year, De Labigarre returned to the Catskills, avoiding the climb up or down the Plattekill and Kaaterskill cloves. Instead, he followed the zig-zagging new Schohariekill Road from near the foot of the Kaaterskill Clove and explored the two lakes and the two imposing waterfalls that lie in the vicinity of the Kaaterskill Clove's beginning high on the mountain, as botanist John Bartram had done in the 1740s and 1750s. He then climbed the summit known as Round Top before returning to his home at Tivoli, across the Hudson.

De Labigarre had established a route that was soon followed by others. In 1795, it was followed by New York polymath Dr. Samuel L. Mitchill, who was on a fruitless search for deposits of coal. Mitchill, who had spent four years at medical school in Scotland and was familiar with the intense interest in the landscape of British poets, painters, and landscape gardeners of the time, gave high praise to the waterfall at the head of the Kaaterskill Clove, known to us as Haines Falls, and for the one known as Kaaterskill Falls, which marks the beginning of a tributary clove through which the waters of North and South Lakes find their way down the mountain. He described the falls and the view from

Round Top in terms that might not have been out of place in a guidebook for tourists on the track of the romantic and picturesque in the British Isles. He wrote of the Kaaterskill Falls as seen from below: "There is something in it exceedingly picturesque, which, under the pencil of an artist would afford a sketch possessing much novelty and peculiarity." In these words, Mitchill suggested what was to become the favorite subject of the Hudson River School of artists a few decades later.

Other travelers walked or rode their horses over the increasingly familiar route, bent on finding scenic marvels. At the same time, commercial exploitation of the region was getting under way. A road for the convenience of tanners using the bark of hemlocks in the cloves and above them was pushed up the cloves to a ragged kind of completion. Sawmills were set up close to the tops and bases of both Plattekill and Kaaterskill Cloves to saw the surrounding forests into timber.

In spite of the increasingly slovenly look of much of the landscape, travelers arrived and admired. Among them in 1815 was Timothy Dwight, president of Yale College, who stood on the brink of the Kaaterskill Falls and pronounced the gorge below to suggest "a solitary, bye-path" to Hell.

Then in 1819, with the publication of Irving's *Sketch Book*, containing "The Tale of Rip Van Winkle," the cloves of the Catskills achieved recognition in the arts. Irving had never visited the cloves, yet the published accounts of De Labigarre and Mitchill were available to him. He had woven his "tale" in part out of Old World material, including Reisbach's tale of the long sleep of King Charles the Great and his knights in a cleft in the German mountains—a cleft that might have been the Kaaterskill Clove.

As Rip Van Winkle appeared, the Catskill Mountains' period as a scenic summer resort was already begun at a clifftop called the Pine Orchard, close to a constellation of scenic wonders made up of the vast view—the two lakes, Kaaterskill and Haines Falls, and a small part of the upper cloves. Plattekill Clove for a time was ignored. Yet a belief that Irving's Rip had actually slept in the Kaaterskill or even, as was claimed in later years, in the Plattekill Clove, persisted. In order to capitalize more profitably on Irving's Rip Van Winkle, the managers of the Catskill Mountain House designated an area on the road which scaled the wall to their hotel as "Sleepy Hollow"—the site of Rip's twenty-year sleep, complete with a tavern.

When Thomas Cole came to the Catskills in 1825, he did not climb the Kaaterskill Clove but followed the same route used by Bartram, De Labigarre, Mitchill, Dwight, and many others to the lakes and the Kaaterskill Falls. He did not penetrate deeper into any of the cloves for many years. The success of Cole's use of European romanticism as applied to the American landscape in its wilderness aspect caused other painters to follow his trail. The owners of the Catskill Mountain House advertised the falls at the head of the Kaaterskill Clove and the view from the Pine Orchard as their greatest attractions. The hotel's guests became a pool of potential purchasers of views of the sights they admired, and so stimulated the production of paintings. In 1839, poet-editor William Cullen Bryant complained in his *New York Evening Post* that guests at the Mountain House were overly narrow in their choice of scenery to admire. Hardly any visitors explored the Kaaterskill Clove—nearly all went no farther than the two falls at the clove's head.

By that year, the range of subjects for painting was being expanded to include the Plattekill Clove. The leader in this effort was versatile Charles Lanman, a painter, author, librarian, and secretary of Daniel Webster. Lanman had recently taken up painting and established himself and a lively group of young friends in Levi Myers's picturesque old farmhouse close to the foot of the Plattekill Clove. From there they climbed the clove, fished for trout, explored Schue's Pond behind Plattekill Mountain, and slept on top of Overlook Mountain.

In fervent prose published in both the United States and England, Lanman praised the wildness and beauty of the Plattekill Clove and its vicinity. He invented Indian legends that rivaled those prepared to please the Catskill Mountain House guests; he told of adventures at the rattlesnake den on Minister's Face, the crumbling promontory jutting eastward from Overlook Mountain; he romanticized the hunters and farmers among whom he lived and whose folklore he absorbed; and he described with passion the many falls and other features within his clove. He wrote of the "Double Leap, with its almost fathomless pool, containing a hermit trout that has laughed at the angler's skill for a score of years; the Mountain Spirit, haunted by the disembodied spirit of an Indian girl," of the Blue Bell Falls, the Black Chasm, the Gray

Chasm, and the Devil's Chamber. The Plattekill, (or Plauterkill Clove, as Lanman spelled it) was far wilder than the Kaaterskill Clove, which, said Lanman, "was fast filling up with habitations of improvement" and so losing its original charm.

In spite of the loss Lanman described, visitors to the lower Kaaterskill Clove were increasing lured by the many paintings of its scenery that were being exhibited in large American cities. Soon, many of the clove's waterfalls were given names—the Fawn's Leap, Buttermilk Falls, and, later on, La Belle Falls, Niobe Falls, and others.

In June 1840, Thomas Cole joined the Plattekill Clove enthusiasts with a letter in which he invited William Cullen Bryant to join him in an expedition to the clove. He had never visited it, but he "was reserving the delicate morsel to be shared with you." In June, the two friends did explore the Stony and Plattekill cloves. Bryant wrote an account of the trip for his *Evening Post*, delved into the etymology of "clove," and described in detail and with skill the wonders he and Cole had seen. The scenery of the Plattekill Clove, said Bryant is "perhaps more extraordinary" than that of the familiar Kaaterskill Clove.

The 1840s may well have marked the height of clove fever among American painters, with Asher Durand and his pupils, including Casilear, Kensett, and C. P. Cranch, working out of Palenville at the foot of the Kaaterskill Clove. Many other painters a bit later haunted farm boardinghouses in the Stony Clove vicinity and spread out from the three cloves to all parts of the Catskills.

After Cole's death, art patron Jonathan Sturges commissioned Durand to create a painting commemorating the friendship of Cole and Bryant. The result, the widely known "Kindred Spirits," forms a fitting aesthetic climax to the period when the Catskills' cloves had the power to excite the imaginations of American painters. The painting, showing the two men deep in thought while standing on a ledge overlooking a rushing stream, is not an exact transcript of a particular spot in either of the principal cloves—the weight of evidence available suggests that it was intended to record a moment in the excursion of the two men in 1840 as they explored the Stony and Plattekill Cloves for the first time.

Painters, most of lesser stature, followed the pioneer Hudson River School men to the cloves. Until well into our century these people worked in a variety of mediums. One of them specialized in painting waterfalls on weathered shingles; another drew falls with a toothpick on the soft underbellies of freshly gathered bracket fungi.

Commercialization of the two principal cloves went on as artists came and went. Bluestone quarrying, furniture making, tanning, and lumbering all seemed to observers from the 1850s through the turn of the century to be foretelling the destruction of the cloves' scenic marvels. Summer hotels clustered at the heads of both cloves. Attached to one in Plattekill Clove was a tourist attraction known as the Devil's Kitchen. There, rustic ladders and bridges and a handsome gazebo made the wonders of the upper falls accessible to all but the very, very timid. A caged bear added to

Two of this group of fashionably dressed tourists look down into the depths of the Kaaterskill Clove while four others stare at an unknown attraction off picture. All are carrying "mountain sticks." This stereograph is one of a popular series called "The Glens of the Catskills."

PUBLISHED BY E. AND H.T. ANTHONY, NEW YORK, C. 1870

the pull of the place. The waters of the upper Kaater-skill and its tributary gorge had long before been dammed up in order that a display of falling water might be turned on for paying guests when the stream was low. Champagne and soft drinks were supplied to be drunk as the falls gushed.

Today, although far better highways follow both the Kaaterskill and the Plattekill cloves and the Kaaterskill Clove is used by more people than ever, the cloves themselves are returning to a kind of semi-wilderness similar to that which prevailed in the heyday of the Hudson River School painters. The cloves, taken as a whole, are monuments to a fine moment in the story of the cooperation of a distinctive landscape and the painters who fell in love with it.

The "Hardenbergh Manor House" was never a manor house. It was built as the nineteenth century began by Lewis Hardenbergh, mill owner, farmer and town supervisor. AUTHOR'S PHOTOGRAPH

IF THE MAJOR'S GHOST
CAME BACK TO HIS PATENT

ATSKILL MOUNTAIN PEOPLE OF THE PAST AND present have reported sighting a fair number of ghosts: ghosts of early settlers, of Indians, of people murdered for gain or in passion, and of suicides. Summer boarders of the last century eagerly listened to tales of local ghosts and so encouraged the region's ghost population to grow.

Yet the ghost of one man who had a very good reason for haunting the Catskills has never been seen. This man was Major Johannis Hardenbergh, who was the front man for the group of eight to whom the million-and-a-half acres of the Hardenbergh Patent, which included most of the Catskills, were granted in 1708.

Ghost lore holds that so strong is the tie between a human and the part of the earth that mattered to him that even death cannot entirely break it. So some people return as ghosts to guard or reveal—depending on the ghost's mood—the sites of buried treasure, to lament at the scene of a murder, or to point out the correct boundaries of lands which they once owned and cherished. Because Major Hardenbergh's emotions were deeply involved in defending the boundaries of the patent that bears his name, he surely had an excellent reason for returning as a ghost.

(One of his grandsons is said to have done so. He was Gross Hardenbergh, who was shot by tenants whom he planned to evict in 1808. Old-timers in Woodbourne, in Sullivan County, used to say they'd been told that Gross's ghost and that of his horse had once been seen galloping along the base of the hill on which the murderous tenants had lain hidden behind a cluster of mountain laurel bushes.)

But the Major himself has stubbornly refused to make an appearance as a ghost. In more than a quarter of a century of wandering about the Hardenbergh Patent and keeping an ear open for local ghost stories, I have never once come across any sign of the Major.

In spite of the absence of his ghost, the presence of the Major and his descendants still hovers over the Catskills. In the northeastern corner of the town of Roxbury, for example, stands a fine stone dwelling known in the neighborhood as the Hardenbergh Manor House. The house was built shortly after 1800 by Isaac Hardenbergh, another grandson of the Major. In its early years, it served as a store and post office known as Hardenbergh's Mills because of Isaac's saw and grist mills on the nearby Bear Kill. Across the highway from the old house is a field, now growing up to brush. According to local tradition, it was from this field that the plant called creeping thyme (*Thymus Serpyllum*) got a foothold from which it invaded much of the northern Catskills.

Isaac Hardenbergh, the story goes, imported a sheep from Greece and placed it in a paddock in the field. Tangled in the sheep's wool were some creeping thyme seeds, and it is from these seeds that the Catskills' millions of creeping thyme plants are descended. The story may be true or it may not. During Isaac's lifetime, creeping thyme had escaped from cultivation in Pennsylvania, Massachusetts, and New York.

Yet it is true enough that the plant has had a noticeable impact on the Catskills, where many hillsides glow by summer with the lavender-pink of its blossoms. The thyme has driven out pasture grasses and supplied nectar from which mountain bees make an aromatic honey similar, many say, to Mount Hymettus honey, which was famous among the ancient Greeks for its medicinal and gastronomic qualities. As more and more land in the Catskills reverts to brush and forest, the creeping thyme population, intolerant of shade, is declining.

Most obvious as a mark of the Hardenbergh presence in the Catskills is the town of Hardenburgh, named in honor of the Major in 1859 and made up of lands taken from the adjoining towns of Denning and Shandaken. As the new town was born, the forests that covered its many mountains and ridges were being converted to lumber at sawmills powered by the town's streams. Once most of the original forests were gone, the cutover lands were allowed to be sold for unpaid taxes. Much of this land eventually went to form parts of the New York State Forest Preserve, which now encompasses more than 40 percent of Hardenburgh's area. Some of the abandoned lands became private estates (the Gould's Furlough Lodge being the largest) or fishing clubs owned and used by urban people who employed guards to patrol their fine trout streams and lakes. The year-round population of the town rose to a little over 700 by 1900. By then, every usable bit of farm land was being put to use in the narrow valleys and on hill and mountain sides where the bedrock was covered with enough glacially deposited soil.

As the twentieth century got under way, Howard Hendricks, of Kingston, wrote an account of Hardenburgh which presented the best and the worst sides of the town as they appeared to Ulster County lowlanders:

> There are more rock and stone than soil, and there is little reason to believe that nature ever designed it for an agricultural paradise. Nor has it ever been among the suspected sites of the Garden of Eden. And yet the general topographical features are invested with peculiar charm. The towering mountain crags and scattered bits of valley, the wildwood and forest primeval, are dimpled over with beautiful lakes and thickly threaded with purling streams which abound with trout. And there are wild and picturesque glens where the true artist may revel in his work without recourse to his imagination. There is grandeur in these vast mountains forests, and there is placid beauty in the lovely lakes. Rarely indeed is the contrasting landscape so happily posed as we find it in this wild mountain town.

Hendricks's words well characterize the Hardenburgh of today.

At the time of Hendricks's writing in 1907, the felling and sawing of Hardenburgh's trees had declined, as had farming. The influx of summer people and club and estate employees could not make up for the loss of the people who had worked at lumbering and subsistence farming. The town's population dwindled until by 1980 it had only 279 people listed by the census taker. Hardenburgh had become the smallest town in population on the old Hardenbergh Patent—while having the highest per capita taxes.

Hardenburgh's troubles were complicated by the reluctance of owners of estates and fishing clubs to pay ever-higher taxes. Some sold to tax-exempt groups such as the Zen Studies Society at Beecher Lake and the Boy Scout camp at Alder Lake. A succession of events beginning in 1976 caused Hardenburgh, for the first time in its existence, to attract national attention. The announcement that a majority of Hardenburgh taxpayers had become ministers of a church whose members claimed gave them a right to a tax exemption—and the suggestion that Hardenburgh file for bankruptcy or submit to being phased out as a separate town with its land and people being divided among neighboring towns—were widely reported and discussed.

It is not easy to imagine what the ghost of Major Hardenbergh would make of all this were it to come back to the Catskills. Certainly the ghost would be annoyed because, while Hardenbergh's name was correctly spelled in the act which created the town that honors him, it soon came to have a "u" substituted for

Thinly-populated Hardenburgh still retains much of its rural charm.

AUTHOR'S PHOTOGRAPH

the "e" in the last syllable. Perhaps this was due to a desire to anglicize the name (as in "Edinburgh"), or perhaps the change reflected the hostility that old-time mountain people feel toward the old landlords of the Catskills. Certainly the ghost would have regretted the vanishing of the Hardenbergh Mills post office. And because from what we know of the Major we can't help feeling that he had a good share of pride, his ghost would have been disturbed at the possibility of the loss of the last survival of his name, if only in a misspelled form, from the map of the Catskills.

An engraving from a water color by Winslow Homer was used to illustrate a story about huckleberry picking in the Catskills and Shawangunks in the American Agriculturist, September, 1879.

HUCKLEBERRY TIME
IN THE MOUNTAINS

WHEN HENRY THOREAU CAME TO THE CATS-kills in the summer of 1844, he charac-terized the mountaintop between the Kaaterskill Falls and the famed Moun-tain House not as the setting of a great summer hotel but as "the raspberry and huckle-berry region." Thoreau often dined on wild huckleber-ries and notes their presence in accounts of his moun-tain climbs. In *Walden*, Thoreau expressed a strong belief that in order to truly enjoy a huckleberry, one must eat it on the spot immediately after picking. He said shipping huckleberries to an urban market destroyed the berry's delicate bloom along with its flavor.

This kind of talk seemed nonsense to the people of the Catskills and the adjoining Shawangunks, for by the 1840s, huckleberries were becoming a significant source of income to them. Picking the berries and shipping them to New York was beginning to employ thousands of busy hands.

By the 1870s, thanks to the services of the Hudson River as a cheap shipping route and the extension of railroads into the mountains, the huckleberry trade had become well-organized and entered several decades of prosperity interrupted only by occasional seasons when uncooperative weather diminished the crop. In July 1875, the *Kingston Weekly Freeman* told of the enthusiasm that stirred the people of the huckleberry country to a kind of midsummer madness each year. In the southern Catskills (the "Shandaken Mountains," the *Freeman* called them), early pickers were climbing four or five miles up the mountains, especially to the treeless summit of Shokan High Point, laden with pails. In a few weeks, the *Freeman* predicted, the mountains would be "swarming with pickers."

Early berries brought the highest price, hence the beginning of the picking season gave a modest gold-rush flavor to the Catskills. Steamers like the *Ulster* and *Saugerties* of Saugerties "put on extra speed in order to rush the berries to market" in that greatest of huckle-berry consumers, the City of New York.

For more than a month, families from the Hudson Valley camped out among the mountains, often in a holiday spirit. They sold their harvest each evening to dealers who waited with horses and wagons at convenient spots and then boxed and hauled the berries to Hudson River landings.

The huckleberry pickers of the Catskills and the Shawangunks were carrying on a tradition of harvest-time life brought from Europe. There, hop-picking in England's Kent and grape-picking in France and Italy brought out otherwise not-fully-employed people to earn some money while enjoying open-air life and fresh social experiences. All the pickers, however, were not members of well-functioning families. It was a time when the advance of industrialization had brought chronic unemployment and had sent men wandering the roads of the country as tramps. Many tramps answered the call of the huckleberry seasons and some were rough and edgy characters. The *Catskill Examiner* in 1880 hinted, in a jocose manner, at the various frivolous ways in which those pickers spent their huckleberry money:

> Now the huckleberry picker,
> Early in the break of the day,
> Girds his loins and takes the warpath,
> Seeks for berries where he may.
> Then in the coolness of the evening
> When the herd winds slowly oe'r the lea
> He comes to town and swaps his trophies
> For tobacco, snuff and tea.

"Tea" in the verse was a popular 1890s euphemism for whiskey, into which unattached male berry pickers often poured their huckleberry earnings. And these earnings by the standards of the time might be better than the average of a dollar a day for unskilled labor. An aggressive picker might end the day with two bushels to sell for two dollars. A family of four or so often earned six to eight dollars for a day's work.

One group of people who might almost be called professional berry-pickers were known as the Schoharies. Once they were nomadic people of Italian,

black and white descent who made seasonal trips to
Ulster and Greene counties.

With so many diverse human groups at work in
the mountains, conflict sometimes broke the idyllic
peace which might otherwise have marked huckleberry time. Often, territorial disputes resulted in hostility, as in 1893, when a landowner warned pickers off
his mountain land. The pickers staged what was called
a "Huckleberry Riot" and a lawsuit followed.

Landowners had one good reason for trying to
keep pickers away. It had become evident that huckleberries flourished best on land that had been burned
over. Then, huckleberry bushes suppressed by the
shade of trees were released into new vigor, and the
seeds dropped by birds had the best of chances to
thrive. Pickers set fires during dry spells. In every
neighborhood there was said to be someone who had
skill in this art. Men like these, it is said, had learned
that a fire started in a certain traditional spot would
sweep up a mountainside, while one started only a
hundred yards away would fizzle out. Once the Catskill
Forest Preserve came to the huckleberry country and its
managers tried to check destruction by forest fires, the
phrase "huckleberry fires" began appearing in official
reports. The causes of huckleberry fires often went un-
reported because local fire wardens were reluctant to
attribute the fires to friends and neighbors who were
regarded in the mountains as public benefactors because their work stimulated the berry crop and so put
cash in local pockets.

In the past, the word "huckleberry" was used in
the Catskills to include a number of species of the

genera *Gaylussacia* and *Vaccinium*. The true huckleberry is classed among the *Gaylussacia;* the blueberry (*Vaccinium*), which is the softer and juicier of the two, has been improved into the large blueberries of the supermarkets. Today, the word "blueberry" is taking the place of "huckleberry" in the speech of the Catskills and elsewhere. I first realized this when I wrote a children's book about a confrontation of bears and humans in a huckleberry patch. The editor changed my huckleberry to blueberry with the explanation that modern children don't know what huckleberries are. She went on to employ an illustrator who drew European bilberries, which bear a single berry instead of a cluster on each branch, and showed European bears instead of native ones celebrating huckleberry time in the Catskills.

Bears—and rattlesnakes, too—play an important part in the huckleberry lore of the Catskills and Shawangunks. In 1964, when Barbara Moncure and I staged a Huckleberry Festival in Woodstock, bears, rattlesnakes, and huckleberry fires emerged as subjects of the lore collected from old-timers. Because bears share with humans a delight in eating huckleberries, the two often met at berrying time. Rattlesnakes disdain huckleberries as food, but relish the small mammals such as mice and chipmunks which gather 'round the bushes when the huckleberries ripen. "Filling up" with whiskey used to be relied on as a "sure cure" for snakebite. Many berry pickers took a jug of whiskey along into the mountains and had a nip from time to time in order to beat the rattlers to the bite. Old-timers tell of one picker who failed to bring his jug to the "huckleberry flat" or

A typical burned-over "huckleberry flat" near the summit of Overlook Mountain in Woodstock, around 1871.

STEREOGRAPH BY D.J. AUCHMOODY, RONDOUT

plateau where he was working. When a rattler bit him, he raced down the mountainside and burst into the cabin of a backwoodsman, shouting, "Glory be to God I'm bit by a rattler. Get out your jug and fill me up."

The days when thousands of huckleberry pickers invaded the mountains each midsummer are probably over for all time. The return of the Catskills' farmland to forest and the protection against fire by the forest rangers have vastly diminished the huckleberry crop. Only the bears and other wild creatures keep up the old custom—a bear was seen last summer feasting in a patch less than a mile from my house in Shady Valley.

There is a way in which lovers of wild huckleberries may commemorate the arrival of the huckleberry season. That is by making a delicious dessert once popular in the mountains under the name of *huckleberry boiled cake*. I give a recipe taken from the cookbook published by the Ulster County Grange in 1939 and there named *steamed huckleberry pudding*:

> Make a biscuit dough of 2 cups flour, 3 teaspoons baking powder, ¼ teaspoon salt, ½ cup shortening, ½ cup milk or a little more. Chop shortening into mixed dry ingredients, add milk and one pint huckleberries, mix thoroughly. Put in cloth bag and boil in water about twenty minutes.

Those not timid when faced with calories may serve whipped cream or hard sauce with the cake. It is best made with freshly gathered wild huckleberries, which will not cook up as commercially-grown blueberries do. And raspberries or blackberries may be substituted.

In 1827 Thomas Cole made this sketch showing the mountains surrounding the newly opened *Catskill Mountin House* still wearing their ancient coating of forest. A huge boulder standing on the edge of a cliff was left there as the latest ice sheet retreated, and beside it stands a windwracked pine while a huge rattlesnake, that dreaded symbol of the American wilderness, hastens to hide from the artist.

COLE'S DREAM
AND THE BLUE LINE

URING THEIR LONG ASSOCIATION WITH HUMAN beings, the Catskills have stimulated the imaginations of painters, poets, and other creative people. And so they have become saturated with lore, legend, and fantasy from which they evolved a magical quality of their own.

If you look at a map of the Catskills published by the New York State Department of Environmental conservation, you will see that the heart of the region is enclosed within a bold boundary line matching in its blueness the deep resonant color of the Catskills as seen from the Hudson Valley. The "blue line," as it has come to be called, is not a charm traced on the land by some poetical wizard in order to guard the magic of the Catskills. It was put there by the legislature of New York to conserve natural resources of water, plant, and animal life, soil, and air, and to promote the economic well-being of the people of the state. The blue line helps accomplish all this, while also holding within its protective embrace the intangible magic of the Catskills.

The Indians of long ago may have felt, as some believe, a magical quality in the Catskills, but of this we have no direct evidence. What we do know is these Indians used the Catskills as hunting grounds. They touched the mountains' material resources lightly, asking for no more than a part of their food and clothing. When Europeans drove the Indians out, their demands upon the Catskills went far beyond simple means of subsistence: they cut timber and sent it down the Hudson to market; they burned forests so that farms might take their place; they turned streams to industrial uses and polluted their waters; they destroyed topsoil; they upset the life cycles of wild animals; and they introduced European plants to do battle with native ones.

By the 1820s, protests against profiteering and destructive use of the forests of the Catskills and some other American regions were being made. Pioneers in this protest movement were the writers and artists who were discovering and celebrating the American wilderness and were hastening to record it before it might vanish forever. Landscape painter Thomas Cole was among the most eloquent of the protesters, not only with the paintings in which he paid tribute to the glory of the Catskill scene, but in one of his poems as well.

In 1836, Cole's concern for the threatened Catskill forests led him to write an almost forgotten poem, which was published in 1841 in the *Knickerbocker*, an influential magazine of the arts. The poem had the benefit of revisions made by Cole's friend, the eminent poet and editor William Cullen Bryant. "The Lament of the Forest" tells how Cole falls asleep beside a mountain lake, obviously North Lake. He dreams that the spirits of the world's trees appear to him and mourn the slaughter of their fellows of the past by "man, the destroyer." The spirits tell of the destruction of the trees of the Near East and of the harm caused there to soil and water. And then the spirits warn that the same heedless impulse that had created deserts in parts of the Old World had come to the New and was endangering the Catskills.

Quoting Cole, no longer were American forests "untouched by man," except by the gentler hands of the Indians; a "human hurricane" had struck and even

> our sanctuary, this secluded spot,
> Which the stern rocks have guarded until now
> Our enemy has marked. This gentle lake
> Shall lose our presence in its limpid breast,
> . . . Our doom is near . . .
> The skies are darkened by ascending smoke;
> Each hill and every valley is become
> An altar unto Mammon . . .

The spirits conclude by predicting that "in a few short years" the trees of the Catskills would be swept away and the mountains would lie in "the naked glare" of the "scorching sun," with deer and squirrels gone, and dry streambeds where pure water had once run.

In his "Lament," Cole offers no solution—the time for that had not yet come. Yet the time was not far off; a growing number of Americans were insisting that their country's natural resources must be protected. In 1872, Yellowstone Park was created to preserve its natural wonders. Not many years later, agitation for the setting up of an Adirondack and then a Catskill State Park became strong. After many barriers had been surmounted, in 1885 the two state parks came into being, and later governmental action further protected and enlarged them. Eventually, the blue line appeared.

In 1848, Thomas Cole died in his home in Catskill. His work in painted images and poetic phrases survived him and helped lead to the complex cooperative effort that resulted in the blue line. Besides the magic of lore, that boundary today encompasses more than 750,000 acres of publicly owned lands protecting watersheds and wilderness areas important to the environmental quality of the Catskills as we know them.

Bolton C. Brown and one of his daughters, about 1907.

BOLTON BROWN:
ARTIST-EXPLORER
OF THE CATSKILLS

E VER SINCE THE DAYS WHEN THE LAST ICE SHEET had retreated and the Catskills were becoming an Indian hunting ground, human beings have explored the region. The Indians, or Native Americans, were in search of the seasonal locations of game animals; white explorers looked for veins of mineral ores, patches of good soil for farming, saleable trees, industrial water power, subjects for paintings, or natural wonders that might attract tourists. But no explorer of the Catskills had so unusual a set of motives as Bolton Coit Brown, who explored the region for three weeks in the spring of 1902. Brown came to the Catskills as the agent of Ralph Radcliffe Whitehead, heir to an English manufacturing fortune.

From the time he came under the influence of aesthetic and social prophet John Ruskin at Oxford University's Balliol College, Whitehead had dreamed of founding an arts and crafts colony. There, a small group of dedicated men and women would lead peaceful and creative lives in protest against the commercialization of life and the exploitation of the weak by the strong, which they saw as evils of modern industrial society. John Ruskin and Whitehead believed that a colony like this could not do well at a high altitude, where conditions of life would be harsh; nor could it flourish at sea level, where the atmosphere would be enervating. But at an altitude in the temperate zone of about 1,000 feet and set in a landscape of outstanding natural beauty, there human life and creative impulses might expand freely. It was to find a landscape like this that Brown came to the Catskills.

Bolton Brown was an offbeat character, yet he was well qualified as an explorer. No matter by which corner of his angular and contradictory personality you may try to seize Brown, he retains the elusiveness of a strong and nonconforming man who seems deliberately to resist affection and analysis.

He was an upstate New Yorker, the defiantly agnostic son of a clergyman who would admit no criticism of his religion. Brown went off to study at Syracuse University and left with the degree of Master of Painting. At Syracuse he developed a passion—amounting to an obsession—with physical fitness. He began each day with a cold shower followed by vigorous exercises. He competed in field sports and established several records.

After graduation, Brown taught art at Cornell University, the government art school at Toronto, and the newly founded Leland Stanford University in California, where he was professor of painting and drawing. While at Stanford, Brown took up mountain climbing.

When the Sierra Club was organized in 1892 he was a charter member. Through the 1890s he mapped and reported his climbs for the club's *Bulletin*, including his pioneer ascents of mounts Clarence King and Gardner.

In 1901, he wrote a lively account of a winter climb to an elevation of about 8,000 feet in what is now King's Canyon National Park. As in everything he undertook, Brown prepared for the climb with thoroughness. He designed and made a kind of metal toboggan on which to haul his gear. And although he had never taken a photograph in his life, he studied the subject and took successful pictures on each of his twenty-five glass plates—he used his sleeping bag as a darkroom. His reports of the trip helped stimulate others to take up winter climbing on American mountains.

Not long after Brown came down from his winter climb, his life took a fresh turn. It was then that he met Ralph Whitehead. Soon he and poet-novelist-social reformer Hervey White were under contract to help Whitehead find a site for his arts and crafts colony. The snow had barely vanished from the summits of the mountains in 1902 when Brown arrived in the village of Catskill equipped with a set of the Geological Survey's contour maps of the region. He crossed and re-crossed the Catskills with the zeal of the perfectionist that he was.

When he was old, Brown recalled that, "It was by virtue of my contour maps that I was able to go, afoot and alone, over the highest ridges and mountains in the group. I scrambled over summits so wild that it seemed no man or even animal could ever have been there. Some were flat table rock, covered everywhere with dry gray moss a foot thick, the same gray moss hanging in festoons from all the branches of the few stunted spruce trees that barely survived . . . I tore and ripped my clothes . . . to an extent that forced me on regaining the region of farms to borrow a threaded needle and retire with it behind the corner of the house and sew myself up before I could meet people."

After many struggles and disappointments, Brown emerged in the Wide Clove, better known as Mead's, and looked into the Woodstock valley below. He recalled that, "It was at this moment and this place that I, like Balboa from his 'peak in Darien,' first saw my South Sea. South indeed it was wide and almost as blue as the sea, that extraordinarily beautiful view, amazing in extent, the silver Hudson losing itself in remote haze. . . ."

A year after Bolton Brown had first looked down from the Wide Clove, the arts and crafts colony of Byrdcliffe was beginning to function on the slopes of a long ridge taking off from Overlook Mountain. Brown did not long fit easily into the confines of a colony owned by another man. He was a born loner and so he built himself a studio, and then a house, not far beneath the spot from which he had experienced the sense of discovery that had brought the art colony to Woodstock. There he painted in a manner that made no concessions to the rise of what was being called "modern art." With the help of his talented and charming wife, Lucy, he dealt in Japanese prints to make a living.

In 1915, Brown went to London to study artistic lithography and returned to become America's foremost authority on the subject and the author of an important textbook on lithography. For years Brown was recognized as the teacher and adviser of some of the country's greatest printmakers. By then he had moved to an old farmhouse close to the banks of the Sawkill, and there he conducted classes in printmaking. With his usual thoroughness, when he plunged into the art and science of ceramics, he built his own kiln and kept records in relentless detail of every one of the many hundred pots he made.

Brown continued almost to the end of his life to begin the day with a cold bath and a period of exercises while getting along on a very Spartan diet and lecturing his friends on the bad effects on the human body of smoking. Lucy Brown left for a career in teaching but returned to care for her husband in his final illness. After he died at seventy-one, his body was borne to his grave on a bier of white birch boughs and wrapped in his old blue cloak. It came as no surprise that he left meticulous instructions as to the manner of his burial. Left behind, too, were many sensitive drawings and prints of the Woodstock landscape that Brown had come to know and love ever since that first moment in the Wide Clove.

If a modern explorer of the Catskills were to stand on the spot from which Bolton Brown first caught sight of the Woodstock valley, he would see a very different landscape and would be unlikely to choose the place as a site for a utopian colony. The valley and the distant hills and streams are still there, but they are masked by trees that have taken over the hillside pastures, the cornfields, and the apple orchards of Brown's day. The

Lithograph by Bolton Brown showing his old farmhouse in Woodstock with Overlook Mountain beyond.

landscape Brown saw was a rich and varied one, given warmth by many signs of human activity and a loving care for the earth on which the livelihood of mountain farmers directly depended. A patchwork of fields separated by well-kept stone walls and woodlots filled the valley and the lower mountain slopes. Above this lay high sheep pastures, and above these, remnants of the wild, primitive wooded Catskills stood sharply against the sky.

The forests that are retaking the mountainsides and valleys, once laboriously cleared and cultivated by pioneer settlers, have their own beauty and value. Yet, so too does the more-human landscape found by Bolton Brown at the end of his three weeks of exploration of the Catskills; both deserve to be encouraged to exist side-by-side in mutual helpfulness.

L.L. Hill as pictured in the Daguerrean Journal,
which Hill edited for a short time.

THE STRANGE CASE OF
THE REVEREND L. L. HILL

HE EXPLOSION OF INTEREST IN COLOR PHOTOG-raphy in recent years has focused attention once again on L. L. Hill of Westkill. For it was Hill who startled the entire photographic world in November 1850 by announcing that he had discovered a method of taking photographs in natural color. "This grand discovery," Hill wrote a bit later, "was worked out in the Catskills within the very hearing of the wolf's howl and the panther's screech . . ."

The excitement caused by Hill's announcement was understandable. The earliest experimenters in photography had aimed at color. When in 1827 Niepce took the first crude photograph in black and white, when Daguerre made public his vastly improved method in 1839, and when Petzval designed his speedier lens in 1840, taking pictures on silver-coated copper plates was off to a racing start, even without benefit of color, and daguerreotype "artists" or "operators" sprang up everywhere. Several partly successful attempts at color photography were underway during the late 1840s, but the colors obtained faded almost immediately. Here Hill entered the field.

Before November 1850, Hill had been known as a quiet, respectable man. He had worked as a printer, as pastor of the Baptist churches in Westkill and Saugerties, as a traveling daguerreotypist, and as a teacher. He had also authored a number of booklets of instruction in the art of daguerreotypy, and with his brother, he published a Baptist magazine.

But this peaceful phase of Hill's life came to an abrupt end with his announcement. He became the center of controversy on both sides of the Atlantic. He was praised and denounced; in a single year he claimed to have burdened local postal facilities by receiving more than 8,000 letters. Visitors poured into Westkill, and Hill was offered, and accepted, the editorship of a thriving photographic journal, *The Daguerrean*. He appeared before a congressional committee in 1853 and convinced its members that he had indeed found what the world of photographers had dreamed of for so long. But Hill was also plunged into serious trouble.

The public reasoned that only a few weeks or months would go by before the "Hillotype" would become the standard daguerreotype, so why bother to have pictures of one's family taken in black and white when the glorious natural color of the Hillotype was just around the corner? The business of daguerrotypists came close to a halt. An agitated committee of the Daguerrean Society of New York rushed to Westkill and implored Hill to release his process and so save them from ruin. But Hill refused. His process, he explained, had not quite reached the point of perfection at which he aimed and until it did, he would not release it.

The Daguerreans then denounced Hill as a humbug. Hill told his friends that they even threatened him with bodily harm. He responded by keeping a loaded gun handy and by borrowing a fierce-looking watchdog from his friend Colonel Zadock Pratt of Prattsville.

Eminent people came to Hill's defense and testified to the excellence of the Hillotype. Chief among them was Samuel F. B. Morse, distinguished painter and inventor, he claimed, of the electric telegraph and, indubitably, of the Morse code. Morse made two trips to Westkill and stated that not only did he see amazingly beautiful examples of the Hillotype, but he handled them and found that the color did not fade or rub off. Yet the anti-Hill forces were strong. They eased Hill out of his post on *The Daguerrean* and kept up a steady fire of denunciation.

Hill announced the impending publication of a book that would clear his name and serve as a guide to his method of color photography. The book appeared in 1856 under the title of *Heliochromy*; however, it left the Hillotype as much a secret as ever and did little to quell the public controversy. It offered much interesting material on the history of attempts at color photography, some useful instructions on photographic methods, some miscellaneous fillers, and an account of Hill's life and sufferings—but that was all. Soon the Hillotype began to fade in the public mind, and the world had to be content with only black and white, or hand-tinted images, for the next forty years—until the Lumiere brothers developed their autochrome process.

Hill went on to set up in the city of Hudson a stock company for making a cheap and efficient illuminating gas from either water or air. His gas, Hill promised, would light and heat "the poor man's cottage" and make the "mansions of the rich more pleasant, more gorgeous and more healthy." The project came to nothing, and when Hill died in 1865, he was deep in plans involving petroleum.

Contemporary authorities differ in their estimates of the Hillotype. Europeans tend to denounce the discovery as a fraud or a hoax; Americans are more lenient. Some believe that Hill stumbled upon a method that he was unable to repeat; some say he had simply deluded himself; and some suspect that the Hillotypes that so dazzled Professor Morse were skillfully hand-colored black-and-white images. (Hill had once studied miniature painting, and his brother who had a studio in Kingston made much of his hand-colored daguerreotypes.)

From time to time, rumors of the existence of genuine Hillotypes made in Westkill circulate among researchers of the history of photography. Some which purported to be the real thing formed part of a large collection of early photographs that was bought by a midwestern university. The Hillotypes would be chemically analyzed and their secret discovered, it was being said. That was some years ago and to this day no announcement has been made of the results.

The strange case of the Reverend L. L. Hill remains as strange as ever. And unless a genuine Hillotype comes out of hiding in some cupboard in the Catskills and gives up its secrets, it is likely to remain a puzzle forever.

*The most recent contribution to the controversy surrounding Mr. Hill appeared as this book was about to go to press. It is an impassioned defense of Hill by Herbert Keppler in *Popular Photography* June, 1994 titled, "The Horrible Fate of Levi Hill: Inventor of Color Photography".

Marked trails led through remnants of the wilderness as on the second ledge of South Mountain in the Catskill Mountain House Park. Here moss and lichen-covered rocks speak of the vanishing character of the Catskill's past.

ILLUSTRATION FROM WALTON VAN LOAN, *CATSKILL MOUNTAIN GUIDE,* 1887

PARKS IN
THE CATSKILLS

THE WORD "PARK" IS AN OLD ONE, WITH A cluster of related meanings. . . . It was long ago applied to the private hunting preserves of monarchs and nobles or to lands set apart for public recreation. In order to qualify as a park, a piece of land had to be enclosed by some sort of barrier. During the eighteenth century, tracts of American land were enclosed in stump and brush fences and used as places in which deer could be confined — American place names like Deer Park derive from enclosures like these. Among the Catskills, "park" has taken on shades of meaning adapted to the ways of life characteristic of the region.

As the days of Indian, or Native American, claim to the Catskills were fading, a new way of relating to mountains, forests, and valleys was beginning to take shape in Europe. On valleys and hillsides depleted of their old stands of trees by the demand for energy and converted to fields and pastures, landscape gardeners were engaged in a double task: they were planting trees for future timber needs and at the same time creating landscape parks for their rich employers.

Their efforts were inspired by the Elysian paintings of artists like Claude Lorrain, in which nostalgia for the classic world of the Greeks and Romans lingered on, given a new flavor by the romantic sense then seizing European imaginations. Exotic trees and shrubs were planted, lakes and waterfalls were constructed, miniature temples and hermitages were placed on appropriate sites commanding either distant vistas or wild, natural seclusion. Landscape parks similar in spirit were to become essential features of summer hotels and private resorts in the Catskills during the nineteenth century.

While it had been necessary for English landscapers to create their fantasy landscapes on land already domesticated, in the semi-wilderness of the Catskills all that was needed was to choose a site and tie together existing waterfalls and lakes, distant prospects, and romantic vegetational tangles by means of paths and roads. The first park in the region formed the setting of the pioneer resort hotel of the Catskills—the Catskill Mountain House, which had arisen in response to a fascination by many prosperous Americans with the kind of picturesque and romantic scenery that landscape gardeners like William Kent, Capability Brown, and Humphrey Repton had provided in England for their clients.

The classical character of the hotel building hinted at the Elysian flavor of English parks. But instead of relying on Greek and Roman culture alone to give traditional depth, Rip Van Winkle and the American

Indian (in his role as "noble savage") were called upon to haunt the landscape. Clifftops and rocks before long were given manufactured Rip and Indian name associations. Boulders left as the last glacial ice sheet receded were named for their resemblance to animals. Profiles of heroes of the past were discovered in those of crags. A spot at which water gushed from a rock face was named Moses' Rock in order to enrich the Mountain House park with a biblical relation. The Mountain House park with its system of wonders eventually included almost 3,500 acres.

For those who could not make the effort needed to seek out the park's wonders on foot or by carriage, there was always the immense panoramic view to be had from the eastern front of the hotel. Below was the Hudson Valley, rich in American history; beyond that was New England with its suggestions of pilgrims, Boston intellectuals, and Henry Thoreau. Sailboats moved on the Hudson. Smoke rose from scattered farmhouse and village chimneys. Wagons creaked along highways over which Rip Van Winkle might have trudged with dog and gun.

To a romantic eye, all life seemed spread out from this climax of the park's offerings, both wild and cultivated, as if to exhibit the diversity and richness of human existence. And beyond that lay the boundless sky in which a life after death might be enjoyed.

Other mountain hotels with their parks followed the lead of the original. In 1871, the Overlook Mountain House put together a park of hundreds of acres and boasted a view that some said surpassed that of the Catskill Mountain House. Its Shue's Pond was elegantly renamed Echo Lake. It offered a splendid series of waterfalls in nearby Platte Clove. With the enthusiastic cooperation of hotel guests, rocky features on the mountaintop were quickly converted into a great stone turtle, a pulpit, a Poet's Glen, a Lover's Retreat. As in eighteenth-century England, memorials to Ancient Worthies like Hannibal were named with appropriate ceremonies, as were memorials to Modern Worthies like the Duke of Wellington and President Ullyses S. Grant. An extensive body of Indian lore and legend was improvised to add romantic charm to caves and rocks within the Overlook Park.

By the late 1870s, the arrival in the Catskills of a railroad and the revival in the United States of a formal way of gardening, against which the pioneers of landscape romanticism had been in rebellion, began to have effects on the resort parks of the region. While natural wonders and a natural landscape were still admired, round or rectangular beds filled each summer with bedding-out plants such as geraniums, achyranthes, and centaureas made their appearance, especially in the immediate vicinity of a hotel. The plants were grown in Hudson Valley greenhouses and put in place by the thousand as they burst into bloom. Sometimes the name of a hotel was spelled out on a steeply sloping bank in front of a house in the kind of centaurea known as "dusty miller."

The Hotel Kaaterskill in the early 1880s claimed a park of several thousand acres. It included, besides much wild natural land, newly enlarged South lake, which was equipped with a fleet of rowboats and had a boathouse of logs to hint at the now-romantic pioneer days. Around the hotel itself, a gardener trained on the estate of Ireland's Duke of Waterford arranged formal patterns of geometrically organized bedding-out plants. Because of the early frosts and high winds of the hotel's site, this kind of landscaping was soon given up.

Smaller hotels and boardinghouses in the Catskills, lacking the space to offer credible natural attractions, humored the gardening tastes of their would-be fashionable guests by going in for beds of canna or coleus plumped down in the center of a lawn, and for maple trees marching like soldiers beside roads and paths. Verandahs and gazebos, from which a hotel's landscape attractions might be enjoyed without effort, became adjuncts to any properly conducted mountain hotel. Because suntans were unfashionable (suggesting a necessity for earning a living by outdoor manual labor), groves of sugar maples, white pines, and other shade trees came to surround many hotels, which were then named Maple Shade, Shady Lawn, or Pine Grove to emphasize their concern with protection from the sun.

The huge Grand Hotel, which opened in 1880 with a burst of pride in its closeness not to a lake or waterfall but to a railroad station (at Highmount), substituted its view of the very wild southern Catskills, which its guests were encouraged to climb, for a natural surrounding park. Terraces helped mitigate the steepness of the land before the Grand's entrance. Balustrades ornamented the terraces, and interconnecting stairways were lined with plant boxes filled with tender flowers of brilliant colors.

Sports activity was becoming an appropriate part of a summer vacation by the 1880s. The landscape surroundings of mountain hotels responded first with croquet grounds, then with tennis courts, and a bit later with golf courses. As the twentieth century made its bow, even the old Catskill Mountain House brought in soil to prettify its rough, grassy mountaintop into a smooth lawn. Balsam fir trees and glacial boulders were sacrificed to the demands of tennis and golf facilities.

By the 1890s, Stamford's resort-owning Dr. S. A. Churchill was enlarging the landscape settings of his hotels to include much of the town in the kind of landscape favored by his summer guests. He used the sugar maples which, as sources of sugar and syrup had long been an economic resource of the region, as roadside trees and to form alleys. He altered a stream close to his Rexmere Hotel into three lakelets named for three of his nieces. An island in one lakelet became the site of a romantic Trapper's Cabin of logs with a massive chimney of native stone—the cabin concealed the electric power-making equipment for the hotel's lights and elevator. The doctor even helped turn the town's highest mountain into a shrine to the mythical Princess Utsayantha, who presided over the romantic side of Stamford life.

As Dr. Churchill was transforming Stamford, private residential parks were multiplying elsewhere in the Catskills and bringing their own style of landscaping to the region. Early projects, like Onteora Park (named for what was erroneously thought to be the original Indian name of the Catskills), were set on land that was partly domesticated but with surviving wild features. In keeping with park residents' enthusiasm for the wild, the natural, and the Indian, houses at parks like Twilight, Elka, as well as Onteora were built of logs or used weathered shingle siding. Within, yellow birch saplings with their bark untouched served as balusters and newel posts, with vacant nests of hornets and birds ornamenting the walls beside paintings by Hudson River School masters. (A shrine to these masters was dedicated at Onteora with suitable ceremonies: the names of the five leading painters of the school were chiseled into Artists Rock overlooking a broad view that had acted as a model for these painters on their mountain sketching trips.) Pleasant drives wound through woods and beside stone walls and within view of the lake, which was an important feature of Onteora Park.

Fences surrounded some of the parks to emphasize their parklike character and to keep intruders out. In many ways, these parks owed much to the Catskill Mountain House Park, from which their founders had acquired a taste for Catskill Mountains' traditions. The private parks were usually owned by their members as a whole, but the houses where each member lived reflected individual taste within broad park restrictions. Each house, therefore, had its own landscaping style.

A Garden Club formed at Onteora carried out in many ways the ideas of the park's founder, Candace Wheeler. Mrs. Wheeler had distinguished herself as a designer of textiles, wall coverings, rugs, and other objects, and as a promoter, with such people as Louis Comfort Tiffany, of an aesthetic revolution of arts-and-crafts inspiration. In a charming book entitled *Content in a Garden*, Mrs. Wheeler described her own mountainside garden at Onteora in which native plants played a decisive part and in which the topography of the Catskills was sensitively drawn into the garden plan.

Each of the association parks had its individual character, while keeping a common love of the wild aspect of the Catskills. At the head of the Kaaterskill Clove, Twilight and Santa Cruz parks were placed with skill and daring on the clove wall, made up of ledge after ledge, with ferns, hemlock and mountain laurel clinging to the crevices and narrow terraces between. The views down and across the deep clove were spectacular; so, too, were some of the Twilight Park gardens, incorporating almost perpendicular sites on which the native vegetation was organized into garden forms. Much dry-walling helped tie the houses to the landscape and served to hold the pockets of soil that supported vegetation against the relentless pull of gravitation and the annual efforts of frost. When water tumbled down the ledges during wet spells, it added to the effect of closeness to the forces of nature. Elsewhere, water was artificially manipulated into waterfalls, pools, and fountains to give its charm to the summer landscape.

During the mid-nineteenth century, a remarkable park open to the public was evolving from casual beginnings in Prattsville. It was the highly individual product of the mind of tanner, eccentric, and congressman Zadock Pratt. Pratt Rock, as the park is called today, is at once a memorial to a man—what is known in nineteenth-century American folklore as a "brag"—and a recreational spot for Prattsville people.

The Pratt Rock Park rises from the highway (Route 23) at the base of a steeply sloping hillside, up which the visitor climbs past picnic tables, memorials to Pratt's dogs and horses, and benches cut from boulders and ledge rock, to the base of a cliff. The cliff face is decorated with many white-painted carvings. Among them are a larger-than-life head of Pratt himself; an even larger one of his son, who was a Civil War casualty; a shallow relief of the Pratt tannery; a bold relief of the horses that hauled Pratt hides and tanbark; a hemlock tree (because it supplied the tannery with bark); and an arm and hammer (to make plain Pratt's devotion to honest toil). There are also carvings that commemorate such Pratt achievements as his founding of the National Bureau of Statistics. A niche at the cliff's base with a carved bench inside marks the place at which Pratt is said to have planned a burial chamber for himself. The stone, as the cutter proceeded deeper, is said to have proved too hard for him to excavate, and Pratt was eventually buried in the local cemetery. After Pratt's death, his heirs felt embarrassed by the ebullience of the carved brags and caused some to be edited with hammer and chisel.

By 1900, visitors to the Catskills turned from a passion for the romantic and picturesque to a devotion to fashionable outdoor sports and, before long, they took up sunbathing. All this had a visible effect on the surroundings of hotels and other resorts in the Catskills. Golf courses and tennis courts appeared; rocking chairs on well-shaded verandahs were given up in favor of rows of reclining chairs set on extensive lawns on which the sun might blaze with all its might and

Harried urban dwellers approaching the Kaaterskill Hotel in search of rest and relaxation could only have been reassured at being shown a feature of the Hotel park—the very boulder they said beside which Rip Van Winkle had broken all American records in sleeping. POSTCARD, ABOUT 1909

from which flower beds were banished. Sauntering along shady paths leading to animal-shaped rocks like the Alligator and Sphinx Rocks gave way to indulging a passion for hiking. Admiring profiles of heroes in stone could not compete with birdwatching (by then given appeal by the Catskills' John Burroughs). Earlier visitors had fled from the Catskills as the snows of winter came near; now their children returned for skiing on wooded mountainsides to which the cutting of ski trails lent an exotic look.

With the establishment of the State Forest Preserve in 1885 and of the Catskill Park in 1904, the work "park" took on an extended meaning to the people of the region. The hotel and resort parks had been privately owned, and use of them by the general public was often discouraged—a bicyclist or carriage driver in the Kaaterskill Park was required to pay a fee. The new kind of park, however, was owned by the people and might be used by them except in ways that might damage the conservation goals of the park.

The state-owned lands of the Catskill Park now include thousands of acres of what were once parts of the Catskill Mountain House, Hotel Kaaterskill, and Overlook Mountain parks. Social and economic changes doomed the old resort hotels and their parks. Only at Lake Mohonk does a great hotel park survive today, with its thatched gazebos, elaborate flower garden, and trails giving access to romantically named rock formations, a labyrinth, caves, and other attractions of the Romantic and picturesque period.

*The two greatest scenic marvels of the Catskills to nineteenth-century eyes
were the view from the Catskill Mountain House and the Kaaterskill Falls.
Here is the upper part of the double Falls as seen today by hundreds of hikers
each year.*   PHOTOGRAPH BY JERRY NOVESKY

KAATERSKILL
FALLS

NO FEATURE OF THE CATSKILLS HAS STIMULATED more exclamations of surprise and delight, more poems, more paintings, more photographs, more accidental deaths, and more debates about the relationship of man to his earth than the Kaaterskill Falls. Today the falls attract many visitors, one of whom occasionally tumbles off a path or clifftop, serving to demonstrate that excessive admiration may be as bad for a beautiful waterfall as it sometimes is for the reputation of a beautiful woman.

People of many cultures have regarded waterfalls as sacred outpourings of natural or supernatural energy. So they have endowed waterfalls, as well as springs, with an infinite variety of guardian spirits, gods, goddesses, and dragons. The Kaaterskill Falls in its own American way has built up around itself a rich body of lore, legends, and fictions that parallels waterfall lore elsewhere, yet has its own distinctive color.

The process began after 1753, when naturalist John Bartram first told the world of the wonders of the falls. Visitors were few until the early 1820s, but then the concentration of public interest on the Catskills—following the publication of Irving's *Rip Van Winkle* and Cooper's *The Pioneers* and the opening of the Catskill Mountain House—all worked together to change the falls from a wilderness wonder of an elite of scientists and aesthetes to a popular spot with a decided money-making potential. Very soon, a rough barroom or "refreshment saloon" was standing at the brink of the falls with a wooden platform extending over the rocky edge. Guides were on hand for a fee, and ladders and steps were provided to make the descent to the base of the falls possible "even for ladies."

In 1825, the falls had the most significant experience in their recorded history. That year, young Thomas Cole painted a picture of the falls that caused a small sensation when exhibited in a New York shop window. A wave of landscape romanticism was reaching a peak in the United States; Americans were more than ready to take pride in honoring their own scenery and their own artists. Cole's painting sent hordes of other artists rushing to the falls of the Kaaterskill and other cloves of the Catskills. America's first native school of art had been born—to be known as the Hudson River School. For more than half a century, paintings, drawings, engravings, and photographs of the falls widened their fame and boosted their managers' profits.

The falls' guides were soon telling Indian legends, some with a base in fact but others fabricated. They told, too, of pioneer hunters and settlers and of the adventures of Revolutionary War parties near the falls. No novel set in the Catskills was complete without a

Kaaterskill Falls scene. Poems by both amateurs and professionals came to abound; the best known was by bearded and revered William Cullen Bryant. Some guides hinted broadly that the deep, wild gorge below the falls was the spot Irving had in mind as the site of Rip Van Winkle's twenty-year sleep.

Well-known writers competed in describing the falls. In the feverish prose in high favor at the time, they told of the double nature of the falls, with its upper drop of 180 feet and the lower one of 80; they told of the "stupendous cavern" or amphitheater behind the upper falls, formed when softer layers of rock eroded, leaving a projecting roof above (it was on the edge of this roof that the barroom was perched in what seemed from below to be imminent peril); they told of the wondrous "ice castle" that formed around the upper falls late in the winter, with its wedding cake elegance of tiers of icicles and Gothic-seeming tracery.

All visitors admired the falls, but some objected to the results of the management's efforts to put their show on a predictable, business-like basis. Because the falls dwindled to almost nothing in a hot and dry summer, the managers devised a way of impounding water above and releasing it only when a group of paying visitors were in place to enjoy the spectacle. Another feature, which the religious-minded felt to be a detraction from the "God's handiwork" aspect of the place, was the lowering from the platform of baskets of food and champagne (previously paid for above) for the enjoyment of visitors. Some guides fired a rifle at the falls' base in order to delight less-sensitive souls with the multiple echo that resulted—this too caused criticism from those of more elevated tastes.

In 1852, the falls moved into their golden age. Then, Jacob and Frances Schutt took over the place, built a small hotel well back from the great overhang and managed the place with skill and intelligence. The familiar basket continued to descend from the yardarm attached to the platform, the falls continued to be "turned on" in dry weather, but such was the charm and human warmth of the Schutts that these crudities seemed less obvious. The artists who gathered at the Schutts' Laurel House became devoted to Jacob, whom they called "the genius of the falls." Schutt often kept his hotel open in the winter when other mountain resorts were closed, and his artist friends liked to listen, as they sat beside the hotel fireplace or Franklin stove, as their "prince of landlords" talked of the lore of the region and of the falls that had become almost a part of his own personality.

Schutt, until he was crippled by rheumatism, took great pleasure in showing his ice castle and relating its traditions to all comers. And he performed another service to the falls: he swept away the many varied names by which it had been known and standardized it as the *Kaaterskill Falls*.

In the early 1880s, the Schutts enlarged and modernized their hotel in the hope of a more elegant appearance and greater profits. The profits did not materialize, the Schutts died, and the falls and the Laurel House embarked on a slow decline. Eventually, the covered stairway leading to the base of the falls decayed, and the falls ceased to be "turned on," as Americans lost much of their once-greedy appetite for the sight of falling water.

Finally, the falls and the house were bought by the State of New York and added to the state park. The dilapidated hotel was burned down, and the signs of nearly all the past efforts at commercializing the falls vanished. Year by year, the wounded earth surrounding the falls seemed headed for a return to its old wilderness character. Yet this did not happen. A new growth of interest in hiking and camping and in getting close to the heart of nature brought a fresh flood of visitors. The popularity of the nearby North Lake campsite increased the flood. Campers close to the top of the falls multiplied until a small tent city appeared. Problems of sanitation and safety made it necessary to forbid camping at the site.

Day use has also proved to be problem-causing. The trail leading from Route 23A steeply upward to the falls base is immensely popular. Fatal accidents have occurred on its narrow higher part. The feet of so many hikers have cut deeply into the earth and the path has become badly eroded. Old-timers say that the falls were better protected under the former system of railings, stairways, and watchful guides, yet few are willing to see these protective devices return and detract from the natural charm of the place.

How can a natural wonder inspire and delight the people of our own time and yet save itself from the destructive effects of the boots, beer cans, and the carelessness of its admirers? The question has not yet found a satisfactory answer, but an answer is badly needed.

Typical of little caves once used by Indians is this one at North Lake. A similar one close by but on the lake shore sheltered botanists John and William Bartram one night in 1753. AUTHOR'S PHOTOGRAPH

SOME CAVES OF
THE CATSKILLS—
PLAIN AND FANCIED

O LD-TIME NOVELS WITH A CATSKILL MOUNTAIN setting make much use of both realistic caves and elaborate, imaginary ones.

George W. Owen did just that in his *The Leech Club, or, The Mysteries of the Catskills* of 1874. He described the plain kind of cave briefly and well: "openings appear in the solid rock forming rooms sometimes shapeless as the den of a wild beast, but often of regular dimensions, having the angles clearly defined." Here, Owen is writing of the rock shelters formed when a soft lower stratum of sandstone or shale erodes, leaving a projecting shelf above. Similar to these are the shelters created when the retreat of the last Ice Age left a large rock so placed as to form a roof across a fissure in the bedrock.

But Owen was not satisfied with these plain cavelets. When he sends his heroes on the trail of a mysterious Indian hermit who has come to the mountains to "visit the graves of his ancestors," they find their way to an immense "dark unexplored cavern in the bowels of the mountain." The cavern wanders on endlessly; from time to time, the heroes catch glimpses, by the light of their pine-knot torches, of ghostly apparitions flitting about. This and similar caverns have a purpose: they enable characters to appear and disappear at the author's command as they pop in and out of the fictional cavern entrances that seem to riddle the upper levels of the Catskills.

Owen used his imagination to good effect in his stirring novel of realistic political corruption and romantic high jinks, but De Witt Clinton Overbaugh, in his *Hermit of the Catskills* (1900), outbid him for whatever trophy might be offered for dreaming up the most fanciful cave in all the Catskills. The cave of Overbaugh's hermit lay close to the top of High Point, in the town of Olive. It was entered through a "heavy low oaken door, which firmly secured the entrance in the solid granite." The interior in the days of the American Revolution was furnished in the style associated with millionaires' hunting lodges of the 1890s. There were "chairs made in rustic style from the mountain ash, all richly covered with skins of animals captured in the chase." A lamp hanging from the ceiling was made of horns "of the mountain goat" and was fed with "oil extracted from the fat of the black bear." A beautiful young Indian woman, dressed "in robes decked with beads and feathers, in the picturesque costume of her tribe," was the hermit's cavemate. One room of the cave was elegantly fitted up as a Masonic lodge. George Washington, Overbaugh wrote, had once visited the cave—his portrait hung on a wall beside that of another distinguished guest, Joseph Brant, the Indian ally of the British in revolutionary days.

Of all the early writers of fiction dealing with the Catskills, only Washington Irving successfully resisted the obsession with caves. Although all the tales of longtime sleepers that preceded his Rip Van Winkle put the sleepers comfortably to bed in caves, Irving forced Rip to take his twenty-year sleep in the open air.

In the *Royalists Daughter, or, The Dutch Dominie of the Catskills, A Tale of the Revolution*, the Reverend David Murdoch handled his special cave problem with skill. He was writing his big, bustling novel to glorify the Catskill Mountain House, whose staff clergyman he had been. While his plot and characters were wildly melodramatic, the landscape setting in which they moved was true to the facts—as any skeptical Mountain House guest could find out for himself.

It was in a natural limestone cave at the base of the mountains near the village of Catskill that Dr. Murdoch staged his big cave scene. He placed sixty slaves, most of them born in Africa, inside the cave during the early years of the Revolution. The slaves perform African religious rites; they sing, they chant, they dance. Their "fetish"—a big rattlesnake—is brought out and serves as a ventriloquist's dummy to explain that the meeting has as its purpose a slave insurrection financed by British gold. The meeting is broken up when a young Dutch farmer, spying on the gathering from an upper ledge, sets off a gunpowder blast.

It is not surprising that nineteenth-century writers of Catskill Mountain novels laid stress on caves. The Catskills had become a shrine of the romantic movement, and nothing was more romantic than a cave. Caves can tug at the emotions.

The caves of the higher levels of the Catskills all conform to the modest rock-shelter model except for a few which resulted from unsuccessful human attempts at digging out mineral treasures. But in the limestone region at the base of the mountains to the north, east, and west, there are many caves large and elaborate enough for anybody. Here, water has dissolved openings in the limestone and produced such wonders as Howe Caverns, as well as many smaller ones. In Rosendale, miners left behind many miles of often enchantingly beautiful caverns after they had dug out the rock of which Rosendale cement was made.

The caves that a hiker or climber in the Catskills is likely to meet are a fascinating lot. Many on the southern and eastern sides of the mountains were used over centuries by hunting parties of Indians; later, white hunters slept in them. And still later, when bluestone quarrying came to the Catskills, these shelters were occasionally recycled as forges in which quarry tools were sharpened and mended.

The best known of all the Catskills' caves was not a proper cave but the huge hollow behind the upper of the Kaaterskill Falls' two leaps. It has appeared in innumerable paintings of the Catskills. Summer hotels such as the Catskill Mountain House and the Overlook House had small caves fancifully named on their grounds.

Caves in more remote parts of the mountains have long served as shelters for hikers caught in a downpour or as overnight camps. The projecting ledge near the very top of Slide Mountain is the highest in all the Catskills. It is sometimes called Burroughs Cave because John Burroughs wrote of sleeping there almost a century ago. Like the well-known cave on the Wittenberg, the one on Slide was given a snugger feeling by being amplified with stones and logs. Caves like these have disadvantages, for they are favorites not only of humans but of porcupines, which sometimes make sleep hard for a camper. In a period of prolonged rain, their roofs may leak. And there is always the possibility of a piece of stone falling down from their rough ceilings—the first person known to have felt fear of this possibility was Peter DeLabigarre. On his visit to North Lake in 1793, DeLabigarre chose to spend the night amid the ruins of a log house rather than trust himself to a nearby rock shelter which he saw "threatening ruin every moment" from its rocky roof. This was probably the very shelter in which John and William Bartram had slept in safety in 1753.

There is one Catskill Mountain cave that remains something of a mystery in many minds, including my own. This is the one on Plattekill Mountain known as Yager's or Jager's Cave. It began to appear in print almost a century-and-a-half ago as a resort of hunters and of Indians taking prisoners to Fort Niagara during the Revolution. The cave is described as having an extremely narrow opening, giving entrance to a narrow passage that drops down into a chamber some twenty feet square, with a smaller chamber opening off of it. Armed with instructions from old-timers, I have tried several times to locate the cave, without success. The late Ruth Reynolds Glunt, of Saugerties, who visited the cave with a group of Overlook Mountain House dwellers about 1906, once told me of having lodged in the narrow passage and of some terrifying moments before she could wriggle free.

In his *Leech Club, or The Mysteries of the Catskills*, George W. Owen concludes by apologizing for having failed to clear up all the mysteries he had described and to suggest that there are mysteries in the Catskills that may never be solved. I hope the mystery of Yager's Cave is not one of them.

A lithograph of an Ulster & Delaware train of about 1879, having made the climb up steep Pine Hill has descended to the prosperous dairy country along the East Branch of the Delaware. FROM *THE HISTORY OF DELAWARE COUNTY, N.Y.*, PUBLISHED BY W.W. MUNSELL, PHILADELPHIA, 1880

THE RISE AND FALL
OF THE U & D

O NE NIGHT IN THE FALL OF 1962, I HAD A PHONE call from a filmmaking friend. My friend needed some footage taken from a train as it approached a mountain. Did I know of a convenient place where this might be done? I said certainly: the Ulster and Delaware Railroad between Kingston and Oneonta had numerous likely locations.

But, I added, there was a problem. Once busy and prosperous, the U & D had grown old and irritable. Passenger service had been given up, and the only scheduled wheels to pass over the line's tracks were those of a once-a-week freight. "Would you like to go along on the ride?" my friend asked. I protested that a ride didn't seem likely. "Leave it to me," said my friend.

And that was how, some two weeks later, I was standing at dawn with my friend and three or four railroad officials beside the U & D tracks in Kingston. I watched as a Chevrolet station wagon with retractable flanged wheels was placed on the tracks and aimed at the Catskills. My friend and I signed documents in which we absolved the New York Central from any claims for injuries that might result while we were guests of the railroad on an inspection trip.

Our station wagon took off in the growing daylight. By the end of the day, having stopped occasionally for the officials aboard to take a good look at a bridge, a few ties, or a stretch of rail, we had traveled the U & D all the way to Oneonta and back—a roundtrip of over two hundred miles.

Before that chilly October day, I had heard and read a good deal about the U & D. I had talked with a lady almost one hundred years old and listened to her tale of the jubilation she had witnessed in 1870 as the first passenger train pulled into the Phoenicia station while she kept a tight grip on her father's hand. But until that day in 1962, I had never ridden over the tracks of the U & D. What I had learned about the line had remained unconnected bits and pieces—it was only when I made personal contact with the railroad that everything I had learned swung into focus.

I realized what a very remarkable line it was. I realized then that the U & D had been more than a mere carrier of people and freight: it had been a powerful force in shaping the fortunes of one of America's most scenic and romantic regions—the Catskill Mountains.

Much of the route that the U & D follows is an ancient one; it once gave space to an Indian trail leading up the Esopus Valley, and up and down the Pine Hill (hence the line's nickname of the "Up and Down"). After white settlement began in the eighteenth century, the old trail turned into a packhorse trail, then into a rough road. About 1800, it became a turnpike road. Later, part of the road was paved with planks.

Railroad fever took hold in the Catskills, as elsewhere in the United States, during the 1830s. New York's first railroad, the Mohawk & Hudson, began running between Albany and Schenectady in 1831 and stimulated other lines to be born. Among these was the Erie, connecting Piermont in New Jersey with Dunkirk on Lake Erie. Some of these lines skirted the Catskills, but none entered the mountains.

Kingston people began asking why a railroad might not be pushed from their town through the Catskills, on the same general route as the turnpike beside the Esopus, to join the Erie line at Deposit, thus linking the valleys of the Hudson and Delaware rivers. Difficulties intervened. In good weather, the Esopus could be a pleasant, sun-dappled trout stream; during floods it could go berserk. The steepness of the Pine Hill and the economic slide of the late 1830s all combined to put an end, for a time, to any hope for the proposed railroad.

It was not until 1865 that surveys, the buying of rights-of-way, and the bonding of towns along the railroad's proposed route showed that, at last, a Catskill Mountain Railroad, linking the Hudson Valley at Rondout and the Delaware Valley, was on its way. After an unsuccessful attempt to persuade the state legislature to finance a railroad tunnel through Pine Hill, track-layers got busy sending tracks snaking their way up the hill and down the other side. Pine Hill old-timers used to say with a wink that one curve on this most scenic part of the route was so close that the engineer in his cab might, if he chose exactly the right moment, shake hands with a man in the caboose.

Between 1870 and 1913, the railroad experienced as many economic ups and downs as the trains experienced in traversing its mountainous route. It lived through three changes of name, reflecting a tug-of-war between aggressive entrepreneurs, each with his own plans for the line. Originally the Rondout and Oswego, the line was aimed at connecting Kingston and Oswego on Lake Ontario. Next, it became the New York, Kingston and Syracuse. Finally, its ambitions trimmed down to service between Kingston and Oneonta, it became the Ulster and Delaware.

The changes in the U & D's name and proposed routes were carried out to the kind of undignified scuffling that was not uncommon in the age of the robber barons. The victor in these maneuverings was Thomas Cornell of Rondout.

Cornell also owned a thriving freight towing fleet on the Hudson and other railroads, and he controlled the Delaware and Hudson Canal, which was thriving carrying coal from Pennsylvania. By 1913, with a sure name and route, the U & D reached a profitable peak by carrying 676,000 passengers and paid its first dividend to its not-always-patient stockholders.

Before the railroad came, the northern Catskills of Greene County had been a summer resort for prosperous urban people. The U & D opened up the central Catskills as a resort for low-income people, as well as for the rich and for a few millionaires who set up huge estates. The line actively went after summer passenger business. It sent out leaflets listing boardinghouses and hotels easily reached from its stations. It extolled the scenery, the trout fishing, the purity of air and water of the region.

City people responded with enthusiasm. They traveled up the historical and picturesque Hudson on palatial steamers and transferred to the cars of the U & D at Kingston. Girls who worked in the sweatshops of New York's expanding garment industry, the line let it be known, could now afford a healthful and satisfying vacation in the mountain country, thanks to low rail and steamer fares and the proliferation of low-cost boardinghouses. Members of staid old American families shared car space with recent immigrants of livelier ways—these new people spoke German, Hungarian, Polish, Spanish, and Yiddish.

Private railroad cars entered into the lifestyles of the millionaires of the central Catskills. These carried people like the Goulds, the Fleischmanns, and the Gerrys from their yachts at anchor in the Hudson to their Delaware County estates. Jay Gould's famous car, the *Atalanta*, which served the railroad tycoon as a wandering office, became a notable sight on the tracks of the U & D.

The U & D built up the central Catskills as a summer resort in many ways. It carried food stuffs to feed the visitors and building supplies such as acetylene gas fixtures, sash trim, and doors to be worked into boardinghouses and hotels. It helped keep the economy of the region going year round by hauling hides and leather, ice and milk to the Hudson. Special trains and cars became a feature of the railroad. They carried people from the up-country to circuses and wild west shows in Kingston; they carried others into the Catskills bound for camp meetings and Sunday school picnics set in shady groves.

The decline of the U & D began soon after World War I. Growing general use of automobiles, buses, and trucks cut into the railroad's traffic. Despite continued freight service that carried food for cattle and people into the mountains and departed loaded with furniture from chair factories and milk from dairies, declining ridership brought financial woes that led to insolvency.

On February 1, 1932, the U & D once more changed its name, becoming the Catskill Mountain Branch of the New York Central, a part of a rail system and no longer a railroad in its own right. It was all downhill from then on. In 1948, the romance of the steam age was replaced by the functional reality of diesels. For the Catskill Mountain people who waved good-bye as the last freight wended its way through the Delaware Valley, up the Pine Hill, and down the Esopus Valley, it was more than the end of an era. For decades, the U & D had been a silent partner in almost everything that affected their lives. The railroad had a direct economic effect when it worked at promoting the region as a summer resort and when it built the immense Grand Hotel close to its tracks near the summit of Pine Hill; its service had supplied farms with food for cattle and horses, cross-road stores with goods from across the nation, and had even carried sons off to fight in two world wars.

The last passenger train ran on March 31, 1954. The service of trains-per-day of the early years became trains-per-week. The fate of eventual abandonment was sealed in 1965, when the through-connection to Oneonta was severed at the Delaware County hamlet of Bloomville. A little more than a decade later, on September 26, 1976, train operation on the Catskill Mountain Branch became history with the last freight run from Kingston.

Catskill Mountain people who loved their little railroad for its distinctive character and its deep involvement in their lives tried hard to save the U & D from extinction. During the 1970s, a committee initiated by the Catskill Center for Conservation and Development succeeded in halting the proposed tearing up of the tracks and dispersal of the right-of-way until an aroused public made it clear that it wanted the line to remain alive.

In 1978, Ulster County purchased the track and right-of-way between Kingston and the Ulster County line at the top of the Pine Hill. Two years later, the remainder of the line was purchased by an association of towns in Delaware and Schoharie counties. A miniature train to carry white-water tubers up the Esopus began running in 1982. Now the *Red Heifer*, for many years a feature of the Delaware and Northern (once part of the network of lines with which the U & D connected), is carrying visitors from Arkville to Fleischmanns.

In spite of all the blows the U & D has endured during the period when American railroads everywhere were being pushed to the brink of death, the railroad has fought back valiantly. Now there is scant hope that the line will survive and will once again play as vital a role in the lives of mountain people and their visitors as it once did. Yet the tourist-oriented cars running on parts of the old track are doing well and are keeping alive the memory of the great days of the Up and Down.

The largest rock shelter known to have been used in the Indians'
mountain hunting grounds. This photograph was taken in 1937 dur-
ing an inspection by members of the Woodstock Historical Society.

COURTESY OF THE SOCIETY

INDIANS OF
THE CATSKILLS

THERE IS NO EXPERIENCE THAT CAN GIVE SO intense a feeling of coming close to the American Indians who were our predecessors than bending down and picking up a bit of stone shaped by Indian hands centuries ago. In the days when every patch of soil in the valleys that surround the Catskills was being set to work growing crops or serving as pasture, farm boys (and I was one of them) remained on the alert as they went about their work for the spear and arrow points, the drills, knives, and scrapers which the boys lumped together as "arrowheads." And here and there in the region there were a few men who had never outgrown the boyish hobby of picking up and treasuring the stony traces of Indian life.

In my teens I knew one of these men. He was Byron J. Terwilliger, a long-time teacher in the little one- or two-room schoolhouses that were then strung out along the eastern slopes of the Catskill and Shawangunk Mountains. Byron was wiry and alert, an antiquarian, a prodigious walker who remained unmarried and is still remembered with affection by his former pupils.

Byron spent many summer days walking from one old cemetery to another, recording the inscriptions on gravestones. The results were published in 1931 in a weighty volume on which he had collaborated with Dr. J. Wilson Poucher of Poughkeepsie. The book remains an essential tool for Ulster County genealogists. But to me Byron loomed large after I had been told by a fellow Indian enthusiast that he had collected "barrels" of Indian artifacts in the neighborhoods of the schools where he had taught.

After I met Byron and was led upstairs in his little house to see his collection, I was at first disappointed. The collection was not housed in the kind of large barrels in which Ulster County apples were shipped, but in kegs once used to hold one hundred pounds of nails and were merely twenty-four-inches high. Yet I was impressed as Byron dipped into his three or four kegs and brought up bits of worked stone while telling me the story of how he had found each one, usually on a ploughed field after a shower had washed clean the stones brought up by the plough and a bit of sunshine had dried them and made them almost glow to his eyes.

Today, fewer farmers stir the soil of the valleys surrounding the Catskills which were the seasonal hunting grounds of the Algonkian-speaking Indians who had wandered to the region. Concrete highways and housing developments are on the increase, and not many farm boys walk the fields in search of the lost tools of their ancient inhabitants. At the same time, recent innovations in archeology, such as radiocarbon dating and other techniques that would have astonished Byron Terwilliger, have helped give us a better understanding of Indians and how they related to the world they knew. The growth of environmental thinking has enabled us to see them not as the bloody monsters too often represented by old historians, but as fellow human beings with a message for our own times as we grope our way toward a better understanding of man and his planet.

No one knows the name of the first person to see the Catskills. Yet we do know that whoever he may have been, he initiated many thousands of years of wonderfully varied association between human beings and the Catskills. The evidence we have today makes it reasonable to assume that this Columbus of the Catskills came on the scene about 12,000 years ago, and that he was an Indian, or Native American, as these first human settlers of North America are widely called today.

The pioneer Indians arrived within sight of the Catskills at a time when the endless changes that shape and reshape our earth had made the valleys surrounding the mountains useful for Indian purposes. For almost a hundred thousand years before, the Catskills had been hidden under a thick coat of ice. The ice had retreated northward, leaving behind a confused wilderness of rock, clay, and gravel from which all visible traces of life had been scraped and washed away.

Slowly, plant life had begun to return and, by the time the first human looked up at the Catskills the once-barren land was covered with lichens, mosses, and stunted shrubs. In response to this plentiful food supply, mammoths, caribou, and other large mammals were moving in by summer to graze. It was to hunt these mammals that bands of Indians, traveling from the south, followed the valleys of the Hudson and the Delaware and made camps beside the ponds and bogs that then studded the valleys of the Esopus and Rondout creeks, the Catskill, the Wallkill, and the East and West Branches of the Delaware.

These Paleo-Indians lived by hunting, fishing, and gathering wild foods. They grew no crops; they knew nothing of bows and arrows. They hunted in groups, for only in this way might they hope to bring down or drive into the sticky traps of bogs the large mammals which they killed with javelins or darts, probably hurled with the help of a spear-thrower or *atlatl* and tipped with points of flint or other hard stone.

The Paleo-Indians have left us a few of their characteristic fluted stone projectile points scattered here and there in the soil of the Catskills' valleys. But their presence can be most strongly felt at a place in Greene County known as the Old Indian Flint Mine. There, the Indian pioneers of the region pried veins of a stone called Normanskill flint from the grip of surrounding sandstone and turned it into projectile points and other tools. Later, many other Indians worked the same mine, but did not entirely obscure the traces of their predecessors.

All we know of the Paleo-Indians of the Catskills is what can be learned from the scanty evidence of the material aspects of their culture. We know nothing, from direct evidence, of their religious or spiritual beliefs. Yet we have some right to assume that, like later Native American and many other hunting and food-gathering peoples around the world, they were animists who felt that all things had spirits which might be influenced for good or ill by deeds or prayers.

A change of climate caused tundra-like vegetation, great mammals, and Paleo-Indians to vanish from the region. A kind of evergreen forest often called *taiga* took over. Since forests of this kind supply little food for any animals useful to Indians, human life became impossible in the region for thousands of years.

Eventually, another, milder, climate came and caused the taiga to give way to a mixed, largely deciduous forest a good deal like the one that covers the Catskills today. This forest formed a good habitat for deer, bear, and the other animals that were the food base of the new wave of hunting, fishing, and food-gathering Indians who made themselves at home in the valleys around the Catskills. These Indians belonged to a cultural stage called the Archaic. They did not use the kind of projectile points the earlier Indians had found excellent for killing slow, big mammals. Instead, they made new points better adapted to hunting swift-moving deer and birds. They left around their campsites their own kinds of points and knives and other tools, which tell us how they lived and what use they made of the resources of the region. Apart from that, we know little of them except that they moved about the valleys, worked the flint mine, hunted by fall on the lower slopes of the mountains, and had relations with other native people outside their home region.

It was not until about 3,000 years ago that the Archaic way of life began to give way to the cultural stage known as the Woodland. Among other Indian people to the south and west, such Woodland traits as using bows and arrows instead of spear throwers, making pottery, and growing corn, beans, tobacco, and other crops had long been in use.

Now the Indians of the Catskills started to adopt this culture. They lived in small extended family groups on knolls beside the Esopus, the Rondout, the Wallkill, the Catskill, and the two branches of the Delaware. They built round shelters with frames of saplings and covering of bark; they sometimes buried their dead in ways that suggest a belief in a future existence; they made dugout canoes and stored corn for the winter in pits dug in the earth and lined with mats woven of reeds or the inner bark of trees.

The Woodland peoples' little settlements were not long-lived, for the soil the women farmed became less productive after years of continuous use. When that happened, the Indians moved on and cleared new land by girdling trees and burning. They often set fires on the lower slopes of the Catskills in order to encourage a better habitat for deer or to drive the deer to places at which they might be more easily killed.

The lives of the Woodland Indian peoples responded sensitively to changes of the seasons and changing weather. When good runs of herring or shad came up the Hudson and Delaware, they sent out work parties to fish; in summer, when streams were low, they harvested fresh water clams. In the fall, parties of men, women, children, and dogs set out for rock shelters formed on the sides of the Catskills by overhanging ledges and hunted the deer, bear, and wild turkeys drawn by fallen acorns and beech nuts. The women prepared meat for the winter or made skins into clothing, while the men hunted into the early winter when light snow made tracking game more certain.

These Indians had no written language—they spoke dialects of a very widespread language called *Algonkian*. They were among the less-warlike of American Indians, yet, even as white invaders began coming to America, they were obliged to defend themselves against their neighbors to the northwest—the members of the Iroquois Confederacy. The language and ways of life of the Iroquois were similar but more advanced than those of the Woodland people of the Catskills.

However, the organization of the Iroquois tribes about 1550 into a confederacy, idealistically aimed at bringing about a "Great Peace," had some unhappy effects on Iroquois neighbors. As the Iroquois felt their new strength, they pushed against their neighbors, and those whom they could not absorb were forced to submit to accepting Iroquois overlordship. The Indians of the Catskills were among the defeated peoples. And something worse for the integrity of Indian life in and around the Catskills was on the way.

Once white invaders from the Netherlands came into cultural and military confrontation with the Indians, and made them agents in their plans for wealth by means first of the fur trade and then of growing crops for sale, often with black slave labor, the Indian way of life was turned upside down and set on a course toward destruction. The Indians, like most other people in a similar situation, were unable to resist the charms of such novel trade goods as cloth for clothing, steel knives, firearms, and alcohol; in order to get them, they were willing to sacrifice what had once been their most cherished values.

Up to this time, the Indians had lived in an enclosed system with its close relationship to the land in all its many moods. Now, the animism that had been so central an element of their beliefs and had caused them to hunt in a reverential spirit and take no more from the land and its beings than what they needed for their own use gave way to a fierce pursuit of beaver pelts to be converted into trade goods, and the hunting of deer to be used in trade.

As pursuit of beaver brought about depletion of the beaver population—until beavers could not be captured in sufficiently great quantity to show a profit—the Dutch invaders turned to a vigorous promotion of growing wheat and putting settlers on the Indians' valley lands. The Indians went through the motions of selling, but without a clear understanding of what "selling" meant. Mutual ill-feeling and episodes of conflict followed. The Indians lost the two Esopus Indian Wars during the final days of Dutch rule.

By then, the Indians had suffered much from the whites' infectious diseases, such as measles, tuberculosis, and smallpox, and from a massive susceptibility to alcohol addiction. After they had been driven away from their old valley lands, they took up living in what had once been their hunting shelters or beside small and remote ponds and streams not yet coveted by the whites. Some Esopus Indians moved across the mountains and lived as half-farmers and half-hunters and fishermen in the valleys of the Delaware and the Susquehanna. One, named Henry Hekan, became well known as a farmer and owner of an apple orchard on the East Branch of the Delaware below Margaretville.

The outbreak of the American Revolution brought difficult decisions to the Indians. Most of the Iroquois took the British side, while those still hanging on here and there in the valleys around the Catskills were divided, with most remaining neutral or taking the part of the rebellious colonists. Iroquois raiders swooped down upon the Catskill region, looting, burning, killing, and carrying prisoners off to Canada. White British sympathizers wearing Indian disguises often joined the raiders—sometimes outnumbering the true Indians in a raiding party. Sometimes the Indians led prisoners across the Catskills on trails they and their ancestors had long used.

The Revolution ended with hostility against Indians on the part of settlers whose families had suffered at Indian hands in wartime actions. The Indians nursed feelings of injury when they realized that the United States government was no more likely than the British to listen to their claims for justice. Timothy Murphy, who had been an effective fighter against Indians during the war, became a folk hero. "Indian killer" Tom Quick harassed peaceful Indians in revenge for the killing of his father by wartime Indians.

Here and there in several parts of the Catskills, as open animosities gradually cooled, Indians lived as squatters. One, named Tunis, gave his name to a Delaware County lake beside which he lived. An Indian doctor practiced in Woodstock and used the herbal remedies that were traditional among his people. After more than a century of association of Indians, blacks, and whites, a mingling of the genes of all three became visible. One group of this background were known as the Schoharies. They made annual summer trips through the Catskills, making and selling handsome baskets and woodenware, picking and peddling wild berries, and working as harvest hands with the women helping out in farmhouse kitchens. Some settled down on bits of unwanted land and established little year-round communities—as at one of the Kingston Binnewaters, to the East of Yankeetown Pond and on Gallis Hill in Ulster County.

By 1826, as Americans were celebrating the fiftieth anniversary of the signing of their Declaration of Independence, Indians were still being forcibly driven toward the Pacific by settlers and troops. Yet, in the eastern part of the United States and especially in the Catskills, a new romantic view of the Indian was beginning to grow. Philip Freneau, Washington Irving, James Fenimore Cooper, Thomas Cole, William Cullen Bryant, and other shapers of American attitudes were assembling an image of the Indian not as a ruthless and contemptible enemy, but as a noble savage with all the virtues that eighteenth-century writers like Rousseau and Chateaubriand had discovered in people living in freedom from the constraints of the sometimes-oppressive society that had evolved in Europe and America.

Before long, as the Catskills became a major American summer resort region, hotel owners competed in luring clients by means of freshly written Indian legends of their vicinities. "Indian goods" were being made in such resort centers as Pine Hill and Stamford by real Indians from Canada or the Midwest to make and sell the handcrafted items so popular with the tourists. Beaded purses, miniature birchbark canoes sold to hold pins and collar buttons, and baskets were favored by summer visitors as souvenirs of the Catskills.

Once the Indian had become a figure of romance and a symbol of freedom and simple natural dignity, local and summer people alike rummaged in the floors of the old Indian rock shelters and dug up flint weapon points and bits of stone tools and pottery. When a large stone, strikingly shaped by natural forces, was found at the bottom of Cooper Lake in Woodstock, it was hailed for a time as displaying a message cut in characters of a forgotten Indian tongue. The grave of what was believed to have been an Indian princess named Utsayantha was discovered on Mount Utsayantha in Stamford. Neither of these two finds has been found to be authentic.

During the ferment of the 1960s, an urge to throw off many of the irrational fetters imposed on humans by modern life led young people to give new life to Indian romanticism. The people set up teepees like those of the Plains Indians, but never before seen in the Catskills, and embarked on lives in which hunting for wild foods, meditation, and the use of hallucinogenic drugs all played parts. They tried to bring back something like the reverential feelings toward the natural world and all its elements that the Indians had made into a pervasive part of their inner lives.

By the 1960s, the old Indian inhabitants of the Catskills were all gone from the region except where they had a shadowy existence in the mixed genes of their local descendants. But something of the caring feeling toward the earth which they had passed on came back to the region in and around the shiny new teepees, and has remained to add its own strength and depth to the current struggle to preserve what more and more Americans believe to be the enduring values of the Catskills.

In that struggle, artifact collectors like Byron Terwilliger may seem to have played no part. They were antiquarian hobbyists whose image of the Indian conformed to the one prevailing in their day, which presented the Indian as a being at once pleasantly romantic and, thanks to a heritage from colonial times, abhorrently evil. The collections of these people were assembled from chance surface finds and put together without much regard to context. Yet, examining one of these collections has its rewards, for there are few ways of getting to feel closer to people whose ways are different from ours than by studying the tools they made and used in carrying out the tasks of daily life—the providing of food and the many little household chores common to all our fellow-humans on this planet.

Byron Terwilliger's collection is available for our study. After his death, it became a prized possession of the Huguenot Historical Society of New Paltz. Much of it is on permanent exhibition in the society's museum. There it can serve to remind us of a tiny step in the process by which the American Indian is coming to be seen as a true fellow being, more like us than the old historians saw him.

And it can serve to remind us of Byron Terwilliger, a gentle and modest man who spent a long and useful life in the region of the Catskills and Shawangunks, teaching children to read and write, rescuing old tombstone inscriptions from oblivion and, every now and then, bending down in triumph to pick up a bit of worked stone that had been waiting for him for centuries in the darkness of the earth.

High on Cornell Mountain this cave is set in a stand of virgin red spruce trees where it is used by hikers and campers. A pillar of flat stones does its best to calm fears that the roof might collapse. CIRCA 1910, PHOTOGRAPHER UNKNOWN

NOTES

Lore of a Hemlock Valley
The Burroughs essay, "In the Hemlocks," is used here as printed in *Wake Robin,* vol. 1 of *Works of John Burroughs,* (19 vols., Riverby edition, 1904), 41–75. The local lore was the product of many conversations with neighbors Craig Vosburgh (whom I refer to as "my neighbor"), Martin MacDaniel, and Fred Reynolds. The quotation about Shaffer Vosburgh comes from Elsie Vosburgh Row, *The Story of Our Family Heritage* (n.p., 1956).

With Broadaxe and Poll Ax
For the background of the log cabin in North America, I used Harold R. Shurtleff, *The Log Cabin Myth* (Cambridge, MA, 1939; rpt. Gloucester, MA, 1967), 1–56, 61–67, 212–13). Especially useful in giving traditional accounts of temporary shelters in the Catskills and the log cabins which were followed by framed dwellings and were displaced as farms became established were Clara Barrun and *John Burroughs, Boy and Man* (Island City, 1921), 14–15, *The Centennial History of Delaware County,* ed. David Murray (Delhi, 1898); *History of Delaware County, 1797–1880* (New York, 1880), 291, 435 passim.; James E. Quinlan, *History of Sullivan County* (Liberty, 1873; rpt. 1965), 171, 546 passim. All are rich in details of early shelters in Sullivan County). Jay Gould, *History of Delaware County* (Roxbury, 1856),

34–35, tells of Mrs. John Harper of Harpersfield building a "rude log-hut" covered with bark, all by her own unaided efforts while her husband was away surveying. The acceptance of the log building as a sophisticated design was noted in "Our Homes," *Harper's Monthly Magazine* (September 1859), 513–18, where log houses are praised in contrast to the "Greek mania" and "gingerbread devices" fashionable at the time. The quotation from Henry David Thoreau is from "Chesuncook" in *The Maine Woods* (New York, 1906), 135–39, where Thoreau praises log cabins, especially when built with "the fur on" (p. 136). George Gould's place at Furlough Lake is called a "veritable palace of logs" in the *Pine Hill Sentinel* (September 7, 1895). John Burroughs praised log cabins in "House Building" in *Scribner's Magazine* (1875–76), 333–41, and reused some of this log cabin material in "Roof-Trees," in *Signs and Seasons* (Riverby edition, 1904), 263–80. For the story of Slabsides and its construction and use, see Chapter 9 of Elizabeth Burroughs Kelly, *John Burroughs, Naturalist* (New York, 1959), 124–41.

Rip's Second Long Sleep

For Roman belief in "genius of the place," see Frank Granger, *The Worship of the Romans* (London, 1891), 58–59. The phrase became well known after its use by Alexander Pope in "On the Use of Riches," an epistle to Richard Boyle, Earl of Burlington; in 1707, the teenaged Pope used it in a translation from Ovid, titled "Sappho to Phaon." See *Poetical Works of Alexander Pope*, vol. 2 (3 vols., London, 1891), 119; see also Christopher Thacker, *The History of Gardens* (Berkeley, CA, 1979), 10, and "The Genius of the Place," ibid. 181–82. Many of the uses of Rip as the spirit of the Catskills are given in Alf Evers, *The Catskills: From Wilderness to Woodstock* (Woodstock, 1982), 313–19. For the origin of the Jefferson-Boucicault version of the play, I used Joseph Jefferson, *The Autobiography of Joseph Jefferson* (New York, 1890), 223–29. The 1930 writer quoted was H. A. Haring, from his *Our Catskills* (New York, 1931), 62. Information about Rip's Retreat was given to me by its owner, Harold Hargreave; John Pike of Woodstock reported to me Walt Disney's opinion of the Retreat. For details of the amphitheater venture I am indebted to its initiator, Kermit Goell; newspaper sources include "MGM Interested in Doing a 'Rip' in the Catskills," *Albany Times Union,* February 16, 1967, and a December 1, 1966, story in the same newspaper.

Who's Balloon Is It?

For the balloon that landed in the Catskills in 1844 I relied on John Wise, *A System of Aeronautics* (Philadelphia, 1850), 246–51 and the biographies of Wise in *Encyclopedia Americana* and the *Dictionary of American Biography.* Among newspapers used were the Hallidaysburgh *Register and Beacon Light,* May 4, 1844; *Albany Argus,* May 8, 1844; *New York Weekly Tribune,* May 18, 1844, under the heading "A Perilous Voyage – A Lost Balloon Found"; and *The Catskill Recorder* (as quoted in the *New York Weekly Tribune,* including the heading, "Who Has Lost a Balloon?"). Professor Grinley's adventure was reported in the *Kingston Daily Freeman,* July 14, 1883. The 1976 balloon ascension in Woodstock was reported to me by a participant, Edward Balmer. Professor Donaldson's narrow escape was described in the *New York Times,* July 27, 1874. Among books in which the crash of the *Daily Graphic* balloon is placed in the Catskills are C. H. Gibbs-Smith, *Flight Through the Ages* (New York, 1974), 71; I. J. C. Rolt, *The Aeronauts: A History of Ballooning* (New York, 1966), 144.

Change the Name of the Catskills? Hell No!

In "I will lift Up Mine Eyes Unto the Hills," in *Dutchess County Yearbook,* vol. 17 (1932), H. W. R. (Helen Wilkinson Reynolds) urges the adoption of "Blue Hills" as "a name that tugs at the heart-strings" of Dutchess County people. Horatio Gates Spafford, in *A Gazetteer of the State of New-York* (Albany, 1813), 9, 13 passim., prefers "Kaatsbergs" or "Catsbergs"; H. R. Schoolcraft, in *Aboriginal Names and Geographical Terminology of the State of New-York* (New York, 1846), 31–38, advocates "Kaatsbergs," which he states is the choice of "certain of our popular writers," whom he identifies in a footnote as Charles Fenno Hoffman and W. L. Stone. J. H. Mather, in *Geography of the State of New-*

York (Albany, 1847), 215, refers to the northern Catskills as the "Catskills," but to the southwestern part as the "Blue Mountains" and as "Pine Mountains," which puzzled John Burroughs, who wrote of them in *Wake Robin* as a place were "there are no pines to be seen" (Riverby edition, 1904) 171). "Lothians" is used in the Cockburn Papers (New York State Library, n.d., 5:36) for the Hardenbergh Patent, and on a circa 1755 map endorsed "A Map of the Great Patent," among the Robert R. Livingston papers in the New York Historical Society. For a discussion of Indian place names, see George R. Stewart *Names on the Land* (Boston, 1967), especially pages 8–9, where Stewart states that among Indians, "mountains generally went unnamed." Henry Abbey's "Ontiora" appears on pages 76–78 of *The Poems of Henry Abbey* (Kingston, 1885). I first heard a version of "Change the Name . . ." from my father about 1914; the speech is presented as folklore on pages 335–40 of George R. Stewart's book cited above. For a report on present-day place-name changing and its problems, see Eric Schmitt, "Ultimate Arbiter of Hill and Vale," in the *New York Times*, November 27, 1986.

The Life and Adventures of Ned Buntline

I have relied for much of this tale of Buntline on Jay Monaghan, *The Great Rascal* (New York, 1951), with its excellent notes and bibliography. I owe much to Mrs. Leo DeSilva, former Town of Stamford Historian, who told me about Buntline's grave and its associations. I used the collections of the Stamford Village Library, where old newspapers, especially the *Stamford Mirror* and the scrapbook of its editor, S. B. Champion, helped by giving contemporary reports on Buntline. For a more respectful view of Buntline than Monaghan's, I read Fred E. Pond (Will Wilderness), *The Life and Adventures of "Ned Buntline"* (New York, 1919), with its uncritical view. In the *Centennial History of Delaware County, 1797–1897*, edited by David Murray (Delhi, 1898), Buntline is not mentioned, although *The History of Delaware County N.Y.* (New York, 1880), between pages 292–93, offers a lithographic illustration showing his house and points out his birthplace with apparent pride. R. R. and O. E. Wilson, in *New York in Literature* (Elmira, 1947), 324–26) supply a balanced life story of Buntline and concludes that his "saga" "remains in a class by itself."

Mark Twain as Onteorian

For "big name" guests at the Catskill Mountain House, see pages 280–88 of Roland Van Zandt's *The Catskill Mountain House* (New Brunswick, 1966); for publicity methods of the hotel, see Alf Evers, *The Catskills* (Woodstock, 1982), 358–59 and 361–62. Ralph Lord and Dr. Bernard S. Kahn, of Tannersville, in interviews helped me understand the relations between the parks and the communities outside their bounds. For Mark Twain's summer at Onteora, I used Candace Wheeler, *Yesterdays in a Busy Life* (New York, 1918), 324–39. Vivid recollections of the summer of 1890 at Onteora were given to me in the 1920s by my friend and mentor, psychologist Margaret K. Smith, who spent that summer at the park. For Mark Twain's letter to *Free Russia*, see pages 194–201 of *Mark Twain on the Damned Human Race*, edited by Janet Smith (New York, 1962; rpt.1994). Part of the letter was used in "The Czar's Soliloquy," first published in the *North American Review*, March 1905.

Steamboating Among the Catskills

For information about the steamboat on the lake at Halcottsville, I am grateful to Guy M. Graybill, Jr., who gave me the basic facts in a letter of December 22, 1975. The New York census reports of 1855 to 1875 supplied scattered data on the increasing use of steam power in the Catskills. Information on water mills, including the hazing incident, were given to me in conversations with my neighbor, Craig Vosburgh, who was a partner in a mill that had changed from water power to steam. The *Gussie Paige* was the subject of a story in the *New York Times*; the clipping I used was in a scrapbook given to the Stamford Library by Josephine Sanford and was undated, but probably about 1885. For Halcottsville history, industries, etc., see Ethel Bussy, *Margaretville: History and Stories of Margaretville and Surrounding Area* (n.p., n.d.) (circa 1961), 117–19. I was unable to find the date of the *Wawaka's* birth; *Delaware County, New York, History of the Century 1797–1897,* edited by David Murray (Delhi, 1898), 509, mentions the boat as then in operation. I am grateful to the descendant of Warren Hubbell who informed me in 1975 about his family and of the fate of Burr's steam engine. I am ashamed to say that I have not been able to find my note of his first name.

Catskill Cloves and Catskill Painters

The generally accepted source of the phrase "Hudson River School" is given on page 1 of John K. Howatt, *The Hudson River and Its Painters* (New York, 1972). "Three Remarkable Cloves" in *History of Greene County* (New York, 1884), 81–83, gives good accounts of the lore and character of the cloves. The etymology and place-name meaning of the word "clove" as used in the Catskills is given in the *Oxford English Dictionary* (1971), in which Webster (1828) is quoted as giving "the Clove of Kaaterskill" and the Stony Clove as examples. A vivid description of the wild Kaaterskill Clove as Thomas Cole first saw it and before a turnpike road had made it more easily accessible will be found on page 95 of Volume 1 of Basil Hall's *Travels in North America (1827–1828)* (3 vols., Edinburgh, 1828). Geology of the cloves is covered in Robert Titus, *The Catskills: A Geological Guide* (Fleischmanns, 1993), 128, 131–32. For a discussion of how romantic feeling affected the landscape, see Alf Evers, *The Catskills* (Woodstock, 1982), 71–78. Peter DeLabigarre's account of his trip to the Catskills and its cloves appeared as "Excursions on Our Blue Mountains" in *Transactions of the Society for the Promotion of Agriculture, Arts and Manufactures,* vol. 1, part 2 (1794), 128–29. See pages 271–79 of Evers, *The Catskills,* for Mitchill's report on his exploration of the Catskills. Timothy Dwight's *Travels in New England and New York,* vol. 4 (4 vols., Cambridge, MA, 1969), 123–24, is my source for Dwight's description of the Kaaterskill Falls and the quotation given. See the Rev. Charles Rockwell, *The Catskill Mountains and the Region Around* (New York, 1867), 182–83, 187, 234, 237, 247–48, 256–57, 289–94, 307, 312, for tributes to the falls by a variety of writers.

For Plattekill Clove, I used Rockwell, page 320, as well as the letters of L. Noble and Charles Lanman (August 27, September 17 and September 22, 1840, on microfilm at the New York Historical Society). "The Catskills" by T. Addison Richards, in *Harper's New Monthly Magazine* (July 1854) was especially useful as a report on a sketching trip to the three major cloves by an American pre-Raphaelite painter who was shocked by the inroads made on the wilderness by tanners and lumbermen and who deplored the pollution of mountain streams. On page 384 of Volume 1 and page 34 of Volume 2 of his *A Biography of William Cullen Bryant with Extracts from his Private Correspondence* (2 vols., New York, 1883), W. C. Bryant's son-in-law, Parke Godwin, states that Bryant and Cole, on rambles in the cloves, bestowed names on the waterfalls and various other landscape features. I am indebted for information about boardinghouses and the Devil's Kitchen to Mrs. Stoeffer, granddaughter of the one-time owner of the Plattekill House at the head of the clove.

If the Major's Ghost Came Back to his Patent

Clifton Johnson, *John Burroughs Talks* (Boston, 1922), 8–12, and Neva Shultis, *From Sunset to Cock's Crow* (Woodstock, 1957), 5–6, 24, 25 passim., give good pictures of the ghost and spook lore available in two mountain towns. For Gross Hardenbergh, see Evers, *The Catskills*, 254–61. My chief sources for the Hardenbergh house are Irma Mae Griffin, *The History of the Town of Roxbury* (Roxbury, 1975), 271–79, and conversations with Miss Griffin. R. L. DeLisser, *Picturesque Ulster, 1896–1905*, 169–80, gives a fine account, in words and photographs, of Hardenbergh as it was in the 1890s. The Hardenbergh peoples' claim to be ministers was widely covered by the press; the *New York Times* (April 10, 1976, to March 13, 1983) covered the story well and its reports were my principal sources.

Huckleberry Time in the Mountains

The quotation in the first paragraph is from Henry David Thoreau, *Walden* (World Classics Edition, Boston, 1910), 57. The *Kingston Weekly Freeman* report was in the issue of July 30, 1875;

the reference to shipping by steamboat appeared in the *Sauger-ties Daily Post,* June 11, 1894. The size of the huckleberry crop in a good season is suggested by the report in the *Kingston Daily Freeman* (September 20, 1907) that Abram Kelder of Rosendale, known as the "Huckleberry King," had shipped 50,000 quarts that season. The *American Agriculturist* (July 1879), 247, reported that the American Express Company had delivered in a single day 1,300 boxes of one-half bushel each to New York from "the mountain district." The *Kingston Daily Freeman* reported in its Woodstock items, August 23, 1881, that eight-year-old Willie Shultis had picked eight quarts in a day on Huckleberry Mountain at Woodstock, and that picking berries helped the "working class." The Schoharies were the subject of many regional newspaper stories. A good early one is "The Binnewater Class" in the *Rondout Courier,* November 7, 1851. For the huckleberry riot, I used "A Huckleberry Riot" in the *Kingston Argus,* August 2, 1893. Information on methods of starting huckleberry fires was given to me about 1948 by Cy Keegan, born on the side of Overlook Mountain. *Eighth and Ninth Report of the Forest, Fish and Game Commission of the State of New York* (1903) provided a brief summary of the huckleberry fire problem and the difficulty of "detecting offenders in the Catskill towns" (p. 22). The lore relating huckleberry picking and rattlesnakes referred to is in *Tanglefoot Tales, Being a Collection of Snake Stories, More or Less Authentic, but Interesting All the Same,* collated by a Keeley Graduate (n.d., n.p.).

Cole's Dream and the Blue Line

Washington Irving expressed in seductive words the appeal of the Catskills to the imagination on pages 480–87 of Volume 1 of his *Spanish Papers and Other Miscellanies,* edited by Pierre M. Irving (2 vols., New York, 1866), and quoted in Rockwell, *The Catskill Mountains,* 162–172, a book which did much to draw visitors to the Catskills for generations. Indian relations to the land are dealt with in "Indians of the Catskills" in this book. Cole's poem, "The Complaint of the Forest," is quoted from Marshall B. Tymn, *Thomas Cole's Poetry* (York, PA, 1972),

100–113. For the creation of the Catskill State Park, see Evers, *The Catskills*, 581–89, and "The Forest Preserve—A Chronology," *The Conservationist* 38, no. 6 (May–June 1985), 5–9, and "The Creation of the Forest Preserve" in the same publication, (pp. 10–15), both by Norman Van Valkenburgh. Barbara Novak's *Nature and Culture* (London, 1980), 157–200, has much to say, both about nineteenth-century American landscape painters' emotions as they saw the wilderness being demolished and about Cole's "Lament."

Bolton Brown: Artist-Explorer of the Catskills

Scattered through the voluminous works of John Ruskin are references to his belief in the effects of climate and geographical location on the quality of work. This is especially the case in "The Angel of the Sea," Chapter 4 of *Modern Painters* (vol. 5, part 7, pp. 175–79). My source for this was Volume 7 of the "Library Edition" of *Ruskin's Works*, edited by E. T. Cook and A. Wedderburn (39 vols., London, 1903–1912). For Bolton Brown's character, I used Carl Eric Lindin, "Bolton Brown," *Publications of the Woodstock Historical Society*, 13 (August-September 1937), 15–16, and personal communications from Hervey White, Raoul Hague, and Alice Wardwell. Brown's "Early Days in Woodstock," on pages 3–14 of the above publication, is a lively and invaluable contribution to the story of the beginnings of Byrdcliffe. I also used "Bolton Brown," in *The Overlook* (Woodstock, NY, September 5, 1931, n.p.). Brown's report on his winter climb was republished as "A Glimpse of the Winter Sierra" in *Voices from the Earth*, edited by Ann Gillian (Sierra Club, 1979), 302–5; the quotations about Brown's exploration of the Catskills are from his "Early Days." The lifestyle of Brown's Zena days was described to me by sculptor Raoul Hague on March 7, 1980. For Brown's preparations for his death and funeral, see Anita M. Smith, *Woodstock History and Hearsay* (Saugerties, 1959), 42–43. I also used a draft of the relevant pages of his forthcoming book on Brown by Clinton Adams sent to me on August 11, 1981.

The Strange Case of the Reverend L. L. Hill

For Hill's early life and his entry into photographic history, I have relied on "Autobiography of the Author" in Hill's *A Treatise on Heliochromy or, The Production of Pictures, by Means of Light, In Natural Colors* (New York, 1856), 1–37. The quotation in paragraph one appears on page 69 of Hill's book. For the story of Hill's announcement of his discovery and the furor that followed, I have relied on both the *Daugerrian Journal* and *Humphrey's Journal* for 1850 and 1851. Hill's appearance before a congressional committee was reported in the *New York Daily Tribune* (April 29–30, 1853). An obituary of Hill in *Humphrey's Journal* (vol. 16), 315, seems reliable. Robert Taft, in his *Photography and the American Scene* (New York, 1952), 81–82, writes that Hill's discovery was "regarded as a hoax to boost the sale of his *Manual of Photography*" and that his daguerreotypes were thought to "have been hand-colored." Beaumont Newhall, in *History of Photography* (1982), 269–270, suggests that Hill may have stumbled on a process that he was unable to duplicate. For the information on a Daguerreotype, "which purported to be the real thing," I am indebted to a conversation in 1975 with Walt Craig, assistant professor of Photography and Cinema at Ohio State University. Regional newspapers on microfilm in the Kingston and Saugerties libraries displayed enthusiasm over Hill's claims and paid tributes to what the *Saugerties Telegraph*, March 22, 1851, called his "high character." The *Courier* of Rondout, in which the Hill brothers advertised, was especially enthusiastic.

Parks in the Catskills

Richardson Wright, in *The Story of Gardening* (Garden City, 1938), gives a good brief account of the past parks of the world (pp. 35, 45, 51, 54, 117, 120, 137, and 173–74). See too Thacker, *The History of Gardens*, 47, 50, 209–12. About 1937, Howard Beach of Trumbull, CT, showed me the bounds of the area traditionally known as the Deer Park, reached by what is still called Park Street. Paul Shephard, in *Man in the Landscape* (New York, 1967), 65–69, traces parks from their beginnings to the English ones, which he states were the models for those that appeared in nineteenth-century America. A. J. Downing, in "A Talk about Public Parks" in his *Rural Essays* (New York, 1853), 138–46, discusses the parks that were, in his day, emerging in the United States. Roland Van Zandt describes in detail the scenic wonders of the Mountain House Park in "The Scenic Domain of the Mountain House," *The Catskill Mountain House* (New Brunswick, 1966), 101–50. For background on the Overlook Mountain House Park, see Evers, *The Catskills*, 552, and *Woodstock: History of an American Town* (Woodstock, 1987), 288–89. George Harding's plan for a park was reported in the *Saugerties Evening Post* on July 2, 1881, as proposed for "the high mountain bluff" in back of his hotel, featuring "the best drives that can be made in that section." Gardener Peter Troy, Sr., is the subject of an informative paragraph in H. N. MacCracken's *Blithe Dutchess* (New York, 1958), 151. The *Kingston Daily Freeman* reported on July 12, 1886, that florist John McVey was about to set out seven thousand plants at the Hotel Kaaterskill. Illustrations in Van Loan's guide (New York and Catskill, 1888) show the landscape surroundings of the boardinghouses of the time in their advertisements. For Stamford parks, I have used the promotional booklet, *The Catskills via the Ashokan Trail* (c. 1930), in which Rexmere Park (200 acres) and Churchill Park are offered as attractions to visitors. I benefited from conversations with Stamford historian Mrs. Leo DeSilva and from the materials in the local history collection of the Stamford Library. For Onteora Park, I have used Candace Wheeler's *Yesterdays in a Busy Life* (New York, 1918), especially pages 230–323; "A Few Words on Aunt Cannie, by Her Niece Jeanette Thurber Connor," in *Dedication of the Ground for the Candace Wheeler Wild Garden* (Onteora, September 7, 1921). For Twilight Park, I consulted Charles F. Wingate, *Twilight Park in the Catskills* (n.p., n.d.). For a recent view of Twilight Park history, see John A. Macgahan, *Twilight Park, The First Hundred Years* (South Yarmouth, MA, 1988). Justine Hommel gave me much information about Twilight; Ralph Lord and Dr. Bernard Kahn of Tannersville gave me outsiders' views of the parks. For Zadock Pratt's self-promotion, I used the *Pine Hill Sentinel* (December 10, 1892), which stated that, "He felt his own importance and delighted to see his own name painted on the fences and printed on large bills" (this when he was running for office). Pratt saw to it that his doings were widely reported by the press. Among newspaper stories I used that related to the rocks were those in the *Stamford Mirror* (August 30, 1887); the *Catskill Examiner* (April 2, 1864); "A Trip to Prattsville," *Kingston Journal* (July 18, 1849); and the *Examiner* of April 2, 1864 and May 16, 1863. Traditions of the carving of the rocks are given in Frederick F. Purdy, "The Talking Rocks," *Four Track News* (July 1905), 14–15.

Kaaterskill Falls

For aesthetics of waterfalls in the eighteenth century and John Bartram's visit to Kaaterskill Falls, see Evers, *The Catskills*, 91–92. An early mention of "turning on the falls" is given by Tyrone Power in Volume 1, pages 426–32, of his *Impressions of America 1833–35* (2 vols., London, 1836). For descriptions and praise of the falls, see Rockwell, *The Catskill Mountains*, 234–55, 288–94, and 332–35, which includes William Cullen Bryant's poem "The Cauterskill Falls." "The Catskills by T. Addison Richards," *Harper's New Monthly Magazine* 9, no. 50 (July 1854), deals in a lively fashion with Peter Schutt and the way he managed the falls. For information and records of the final phase of the Laurel House and the waterfall attached, I am indebted to its final manager, Mrs. Virginia Cardinale, of Haines Falls. A good deal of fact, fiction, and reprints of many writers about the falls, including Cooper and Irving, is included in R. L. DeLisser's *Picturesque Catskills* (rpt. Cornwallville, NY, 1967), 41–60, as well as in Rockwell, cited above. For a report of a death at the falls, see the *Woodstock Townsman* (October 14, 1971); for a remarkable recovery from an eighty-foot fall, see page 30 of Rockwell, above; for a denial of rumored death and injuries by the falls, see the *Catskill Examiner* (July 21, 1860); and for provision of "attentive guides at all hours," see the advertisement "Not True" in the Greene County *Whig*, July 31, 1852. I base the final three paragraphs of this essay on ˌpersonal observation.

Some Caves of the Catskills, Plain and Fancied

Quotations here are from George W. Owen, *The Leech Club* (New York, 1874), 5, 266–70, where the Catskills are depicted as being believed to possess endless labyrinthine caverns that enable characters "to traverse at pleasure the bowels of the mountains." Overbaugh's novel appears to have been inspired by Owen's but presents eighteenth-century life in Ulster County in the ruffles and powdered-wig manner popular among novelists around the turn of the century. Overbaugh's cave scenes will be found on pages 162–65. The cave scenes of Murdoch's book take place on pages 94–103 and 363–69. Of the three books, Murdoch's was apparently the most popular. Its first edition was titled *The Dutch Dominie of the Catskills*; the second edition was titled *The Royalists Daughter or the Dutch Dominie of the Catskills*. Copies of both editions in local collections show every evidence of having been frequently read, while the other two books are in almost mint condition. Paul Shephard, in his *Man in the Landscape* (New York, 1967), 168–69, gives expression to the appeal of caves to the unconscious and their place in Gothic novels. Sigmund Freud, in *A General Introduction to Psychoanalysis* (New York, 1920), 128, deals with the sexual symbolism of caves and other cavities. For a no-nonsense approach to the caves of the Catskills and their limestone country to the north and northeast, see Clay Perry, *Underground Empire Wonders and Tales of New York Caves* (New York, 1948), 143–57, passim. For some examples of the rock shelters or "cabins" used by Indians, see "Indians of the Catskills" in this book, and Evers, *Woodstock*, 9–13. My source for Peter DeLabigarre's cave on North Mountain is his "Excursions on our Blue Mountains" in *Transactions of the New York Society for the Promotion of Agriculture, Arts and Manufactures* (1794, vol. 1, part 4), 124–39. Ruth Reynolds Glunt was my informant about her bad moment in Yager's Cave. For anyone interested in both caves and gardening, Naomi Miller's *Heavenly Caves* (New York, 1982), with its wealth of information about domesticated caves, will be a delight.

The Rise and Fall of the U & D
Here I used Gerald M. Best, *The Ulster and Delaware Railroad Through the Catskills* (San Marino, CA, 1972), which gives a detailed history of the line as seen by a noted railroad buff. For earlier attempts at railroads in the Catskills, see Evers, *The Catskills*, 388–89. For antagonism aroused by the bonding of towns for building the U & D, see "Bonding Towns and Corrupt Politics" in *Olde Ulster*, vol. 6 (Kingston, 1910), 321–29. In *The Catskills*, 464–66, I tell of the struggles for control of the line by Thomas Cornell and opponents. F. D. Westbook, in his *Historical Sketches: The Old Senate House* (Kingston, 1884), 34–35, reflects the accepted belief that the U & D had been a prime mover in building up the tourist industry of the Catskills. For extensions of the line and service in its final years, see Evers, *The Catskills*, 550, 557. The tall tale about the Horseshoe Curve on the U & D was told to me by Melvin Mayes in Townsend Hollow on September 21, 1968.

Indians in the Catskills
I owe information about Byron Terwilliger to a former pupil of his, M. W. Wetterau, and to Ulster County Historian Kenneth E. Hasbrouck, Sr. Sources for Indians of the region were Leonard Eisenberg, *Paleo-Indian Settlement Pattern in the Hudson and Delaware River Drainages* (Ringe, NH, 1978), 19–20, 122; Robert E. Funk, "The West Athens Hill Site," in William A. Ritchie and Robert E. Funk, *Aboriginal Settlement Patterns in the North-East* (Albany, 1973), 37–51; Robert E. Funk, *Recent Contributions to Hudson Valley Prehistory* (Albany, 1976), especially pp. 277–78, 279–80, 302, 304. William A. Ritchie, "The Indian in His Environment," *The Conservationist* (December–January 1955–1956), 23–27, gave me a good overview of the Indians of New York State and their ways of life. For Indian-white relations of the seventeenth century, I used Michael Kammen, *Colonial New york—A History* (New York, 1975), 67–69, and E. M. Ruttenber, *Indian Tribes of Hudson's River* (Albany, 1872), 94, 95 passim., which is still useful because of its reliance on contemporary sources. Usefull too is Augustus H.

Van Buren's *A History of Ulster County Under the Dominion of the Dutch* (Kingston, 1923), in which the Indians of the region, for the first time, were seen with sympathy by a local historian (see especially pages 1–19). Also useful was *Many Trails: Indians of the Lower Hudson Valley,* edited by C. C. Braverman (Katonah, NY, 1983), which presents a broad and well-illustrated view of the Algonkian-speaking Indians, who were neighbors of those who hunted in the Catskills, from the Woodland stage to the present.

INDEX

THE CATSKILL CENTER FOR CONSERVATION AND DEVELOPMENT

In Catskill Country was produced with the cooperation of The Catskill Center for Conservation and Development. Founded in 1969 as a nonprofit corporation, The Catskill Center for Conservation and Development is the sole region-wide advocate for the environmental and economic health of America's "first wilderness," the Catskill Mountain region of New York State, which includes Delaware, Greene, Otsego, Sullivan, Schoharie and Ulster counties. The Center uses education, advocacy, model projects and legal action to protect the Catskills' natural and cultural assets, which include the 700,000-acre Catskill Park and the nation's largest municipal water supply system.

The mission of the Center is to build a framework for environmental protection and sustainable economic development consonant with the Catskills' cultural identity; it engages towns and partner environmental organizations in conservation work with a variety of constituencies, including citizens, farmers, businesses and recreational interests. The Center is a membership organization; individual contributions provide a significant source of revenue. Additional support is provided by the New York State Council on the Arts and private foundations. For more information, call the Center at (914) 586-2611.